# *Becoming Royal*

Every family has a story;
Welcome to mine.

Susan Taylor

*A sentimental journey down
the road my father traveled*

SUSAN TAYLOR
TERRY HICKS

# Endorsements

I highly recommend *Becoming Royal,* a great read in a man's true story of redemption set against the backdrop of the poverty of his circumstances, his location, and family in the still-changing South of the 1920s and 1930s. The authors carefully expand the reader's understanding of the time and place by interpreting local, national, and world events into the narrative. The tale starts with the question of who Royal was and takes the reader on an unexpected journey to a satisfying conclusion. If you enjoyed Rick Bragg's "Eva's Man," you will enjoy this, too.

-Rebecca Marshall Farnbach
Author of *Dancing With Prayers in My Feet*
and *James L. Phillips, M.D., D.D.* and coauthor
of six books in Arcadia's Images of America Series.


The authors have brought emotion and drama into this biography that draws you in on the very first page. *Becoming Royal* is an excellent book that I definately recommend.

-Phillip Hoss
Entertainment Business Consultant/
Certified Life Coach

*Becoming Royal* is one man's survival and redemption story, as told by his daughters, based on shocking information they discover about him after his death. Meticulously researched and masterfully woven, it is set against a backdrop of the Great Depression, World War 2, and the Baby Boom years in America. The twists and turns had me holding my breath, as must have the girl's father while living his remarkable life, ever hoping that the secret of his youth would not be revealed.

-Elaine Klonicki
Author of *All on Account of You: A True WW2 Love Story*


When Royal Scott Wadsworth died unexpectedly of a heart attack not only was he a WW2 Vet, devoted husband and father of four young daughters, but he also harbored some deep dark secrets of youthful transgressions which had led to a period of a clandestine existence of life on the lam. Years later the girls embarked on a journey to uncover the remarkable truth about their father. This book chronicles that journey. Hope you enjoy the trip. I know I did.

-Kingsley Wood
Senior Vice President CBS Program Practices (Ret)

Charleston, SC
www.PalmettoPublishing.com

Becoming Royal
Copyright © 2022 by Susan Taylor & Terry Hicks

All rights reserved
No portion of this book may be reproduced, stored in a retrieval system, or transmitted in any form by any means–electronic, mechanical, photocopy, recording, or other–except for brief quotations in printed reviews, without prior permission of the author.

First Edition

Paperback: 979-8-8229-0311-1
eBook: 979-8-8229-0312-8

# Dedication

*To our parents, Royal & Dee:
There are not enough words to express the
praise and gratitude they both deserve.
As long as their memories are kept alive they
will continue to touch future generations.*

*Our dad's namesakes who proudly bear his name:
Thomas Scott, Nicholas Scott, Travis Scott,
Kalao Scott, and Royal Scott.*

*Our family:
Many of Dad's grandchildren have expressed the same
sentiment—if there is one person they wish they could
have known, it would have been Grandpa Roy.*

*This book was written so they can know
and appreciate who he was.*

## 1971

My mother met me at the front door with a glass of water and a pill. I think it was a tranquilizer.

"Your dad had a heart attack." She said it as if she didn't believe it herself. "He's gone."

I saw him just hours earlier; strong and fit, but sometime during the evening, he complained about heartburn, made himself an old home remedy—baking soda and vinegar—drank it and sat down on the sofa. A sharp pain gripped his chest. Mom called 911.

His heart beat for 56 years, then in the ambulance . . . silence. I was in shock. We were all in shock. He was gone.

As the days, weeks, and years trolled by, Mom marched us four girls on through graduations, weddings, and babies, but there's an emptiness that lingers in your heart when you lose someone without warning—an emptiness that longs for every missed experience, conversation, and the chance to say *good-bye*.

Did he know how much I loved him? Did I thank him enough for his hard work and the beautiful, safe, happy life he provided us?

Why didn't I ask him more about his life growing up?

The questions still lingered when our dad's sister, Aunt Evelyn revealed a secret that changed everything we thought we knew about him.

# Chapter 1

> "It doesn't matter who my father was.
> It matters who I remember he was."
> -Anne Sexton

## 1993

The cool autumn air was no match for the warmth we felt inside the car as it sped along the interstate en route to St. Louis International Airport. Terry and I chatted with excitement, and the volume of our laughter rose as each childhood memory was tossed around like an old, worn-out rag doll. It was apparent we value our time together and share a special bond common only between sisters.

We boarded the aircraft with great anticipation of what this weekend adventure might bring. The plane taxied into position, pausing to wait for permission to take off. After a brief hesitation, we raced forward down the runway, gracefully ascending into a ballroom of waltzing clouds.

Though both of us were thirty-something, I reached for Terry's hand and held on tight just like we did as children when we rode a roller coaster.

The plane leveled out, we loosened our grip, and I broke the silence, "Dad was a fugitive?" I tried to reason.

Our mom never wanted us to know that part of our father's past. She came from a generation where people didn't air their dirty laundry—only laundry that's been washed and dried.

I watched as we sailed through the sea of blue, then closed my eyes as a tide of possible answers washed over me. "What if he killed someone? What if . . ."

We "what if'd" for two hours until the intercom crackled with instructions from the flight attendant, "Please fasten your seat belts. We are beginning our descent into Charlotte."

There was a jolt as the tires hit the pavement, reconnecting once again to the ground. In some small way, we too were hoping to reconnect with a family we knew little about.

Our older sister, Donna, had already arrived and met us with a rental car and the three of us headed for our destination—Gastonia, North Carolina—the small town where our father had spent his later childhood years.

This was our first trip to North Carolina. As we passed through the countryside, we tried to imagine what his life was like growing up in this small southern town. We made our final turn into a gravel drive. Leaves crackled underfoot as we emerged onto the front lawn, and though tired from the trip, the fresh country air revived us.

There on the front porch sat our Aunt Evelyn, swaying softly on a swing. She was a petite woman with dark brown hair, but the spark in her eye let us know immediately that she had a feisty streak. Though the evidence of her many years was apparent, her mind seemed quick and sharp. Her aphorisms were uniquely southern as they spewed from her mouth with ease.

We were just little girls the last time our faces graced hers. If we were to have passed on the street, none would have been the wiser.

Her smile was warm and inviting. Hugs and greetings were freely exchanged. It felt good to be reacquainted once again. Her home was simple and modest. She was not a woman of means—at least not in a worldly sense. It was visibly clear to all who entered what she valued most. The dimly lit walls were adorned with pictures of her most prized possessions—her family. The well-worn furniture put us at ease as we settled in for our visit.

We were amused by her spryness and the way in which she served our lunch. She looked like a little blackjack dealer, as she seated us around the table, then proceeded to deal us each two slices of bread, a slice of ham, then a slice of cheese.

As we began to assemble our sandwiches, her tone turned somber, and her southern drawl seemed more pronounced.

One by one, she looked us each in the eye and then confessed, "Y'all know we come from a long line of thieves and murderers, don't ya?"

> *"Tell me about the South. What's it like there?*
> *What do they do there? Why do they live there?*
> *Why do they live at all?"*
> -William Faulkner

Before the convenience of home computers, I spent long hours at the Los Angeles Mormon Temple. We are not Mormon, but their Family History Room had reels of microfilm records and volunteer workers willing to assist filling in the branches of our family tree. It was my first attempt to know more about the hardworking, quiet, gentle father we lost prematurely.

I pulled out several reels of microfilm from his birthplace—Charlotte, North Carolina—and studied the census from the late 1800s into the turn of the century.

We knew Dad's mother, Grandma Bessie. She came from North Carolina to visit every summer when we were young, but we only had a name for his father—John Wadsworth.

"He died in a car accident when you were five." That's all Dad's mother told him. Then she shut her lips tighter than a clam and kept the unspoken truth hidden inside like a precious pearl.

## 1865–1900

After the Civil War, a new South emerged from the wreckage left behind. Textile mills sprang up all over the region, and any hopes of wealth were directly tied to the whirling of spindles and the beating of looms. Though farming was still the mainstay of most southern families until well into the twentieth century, in the area known as the Piedmont, a new era was ushered in. This land of gently rolling hills was quickly fading into the sunset as railroad tracks and mill villages began to change the landscape of the countryside.

Concord, North Carolina, became known as the land flowing with milk and honey, and just like the Promised Land, it too brought great hopes for a new and better way of life to all who entered—all except those who entered by way of the mill village.

Boxcars from Charlotte arrived in Concord filled with the white gold of the South—cotton. A new culture was on the horizon. The mills brought great prosperity to businessmen and professionals, and no town felt it more than Concord. It was agreed by many to be *a goodly place to dwell.*

Dad's mother, Bessie, was born in Concord in 1894. She was the youngest of the four children born to the union of Charlie and Elizabeth Kinley. Their farm on Dutch Buffalo Creek overlooked the mills sprouting up in the Appalachia Valley in the early 1900s. Labor scouts came visiting singing the praises of factory work and persuaded poor white farmers like Charlie to trade tending the land for tending machines in the cotton mills. *Public work* they called it. They purchased family labor as a package, so the Kinley family became first generation mill workers.

Farm work was hard and certainly had its challenges, but mill work took a different kind of toll, squeezing the life out of its victims. Small farmers like Charlie and many others thought they had found the path to a better way of life for themselves and their families, but they soon discovered the road led only to hardship and poverty.

Elizabeth was 58 when she died and left Charlie to raise 15-year-old Bessie. Charlie and Bessie both worked in the mill and lived in the mill village—rows of look-alike houses the mill boss provided for their workers. They were small, flimsy one-story frame structures with little landscape and a lot of dirt.

The village maintained a distinctively rural appearance. Many of the farmers brought remnants from their lives on the farm. It wasn't uncommon to wake up in the morning and find Addy Brook's milk cow standing in the front yard, or the Meyer's chickens pecking at the screen door. Some families had vegetable gardens and shared what they grew. They drew their water from a common well and used an outhouse in the backyard. They had their own churches and held emotional revivals. They helped each other through bad times.

In the winter, the roads were muddy, even impassable at times. As winter gave way to spring, and spring gave way to summer, the mud dried, and the dust blew. Then summer gave way to fall, and the cycle started over again, from mud to dust back to mud again.

The merchants and professional people whose businesses prospered on South Union Street walked a short distance to their homes on North Union Street where their wealth found its finest architectural expression in the lovely two-story Queen Anne, Italianate, and Federalist homes.

James Cannon owned one of the largest textile mills in the South. William Means, the former mayor, who became a well-known criminal lawyer, and his wife, Cora, lived next door. Next to them, Judge Montgomery's home had front doors made of highly polished walnut. Each door had a beveled plate glass etched with a scroll design and the initials "WJM" in the center. The lawns were all well-groomed. The roses looked as if they were competing for a prize while fragrant blossoms cheered them on.

A broad front porch draped around the stately Wadsworth residence at 100 North Union Street. Colonel Wadsworth left Charlotte in the late 1800s and opened a dry goods store with the Cannon brothers—Cannon, Fetzer, & Wadsworth Mercantile. He also owned Corl-Wadsworth Livery Stable and co-owned Wadsworth-Yorke Hardware with his neighbor Felix Yorke. The colonel was bigger than life. He stammered when he talked, but his talk was fascinating. He was well respected, and people regularly sought his advice; however, when he and his cronies spent the evening at the saloon, the mothers on North Union Street would gather their children safely in, as the men were known for shooting out the streetlamps after a few too many brandies.

The colonel and his wife, Willie, had four children who were also well-known in town. Their daughter, Mary Virginia's photograph often graced the society page of the local newspaper. Their son, William, was a prominent physician, and Charles was one of the town's leading dentists. Their youngest son, John, was my Grandmother Bessie's age. He worked as an assistant at Gibson's Drug Store.

The details on the census began to paint a picture of residential segregation from the Kinley family's mill village to the Wadsworth's professional neighborhood on North Union Street, and as I studied this more, it was clear that marriage across those class lines was strictly taboo.

Before telephones, radios, or televisions, there was a telegraph service. Gibson's Drug Store owned a set of weather flags. Every morning about ten o'clock Western Union delivered a wire from the weather bureau in Washington, D.C. As soon as the report came through, the proper flag was selected and flown on a twenty-five-foot pole on the street corner out front. The locals knew whether to expect rain or shine. They relied on Gibson's not only for their medicine and supplies, but for their weather forecast and socializing. Local businessmen and farmers sat in the corner smoking cigars and chewing the fat. Politics and town festivities were discussed. There was often a wit in the crowd sharing comic stories. They shared in each other's joys and sorrows and developed bonds of friendship with their neighbors. Young people often gathered around a phonograph on the counter to listen to a John Phillip Sousa march.

John Wadsworth worked at Gibson's after school and on Saturdays dusting the shelves, doing chores and learning weights, measures, and symbols to become a future pharmacist. Perhaps it was Gibson's where John first noticed Bessie. After all, a magazine article described him as, "a popular young man, well-liked by all who knew him," and Aunt Evelyn said people called Bessie, "the prettiest girl in Concord." No doubt she turned John's head, and he didn't care that she worked in the mill. The two young lovers broke society's rules, but his parents strictly enforced them.

Wherever they met, however they met, 16-year-old Bessie was soon pregnant with John's child. John was 15. Tensions, no doubt, ran deep when Bessie walked down Union Street with her baby, Lola Mae. Voices giggling, "cotton mill trash," and whispers echoing "lint head" followed her up and down the aisles of Gibson's hovering over like a black cloud. The lint from the hot dusty air of the mill that settled on Bessie's hair and skin marked her as a mill worker. Her child was guilty by association and also classified inferior. John's family would never accept Bessie or her child into their family, and an illegitimate baby was a disgrace in her own community as well.

Lola Mae was two and a half when she developed a fever that

led to her coughing fits and gasping for air. John's name is on her death certificate as the person there with her when infection and whooping cough took her last breath.

There was a lack of medicine and medical care in those days, especially in the mill villages. Apparently young John's job at Gibson's Drug Store didn't give him access to the limited birth control methods available. Bessie was eight months pregnant with her second child when she laid her first child to rest next to her own mother, Elizabeth. Bessie then gave birth to a baby boy. He only lived two days. She laid him to rest alongside his sister and grandmother.

A year and a half later, December winds blew and Bessie's stomach once again protruded from her coat as she left the mill early and sent her sister Ella to get the midwife, Granny Mae.

The average millworker couldn't afford the fees doctors charged, so they turned to granny-midwives and healers to birth their babies. Black women were excluded from working in the mills, but they were welcomed with open arms, even held in high esteem, by those of child-bearing years.

Bessie's labor pains increased in intensity as they lit a kerosene lamp, put water on to boil, and waited. Fire crackled in the wood stove while Granny Mae put a little snuff in something like a drinking straw. The practice called *quilling* was passed down from generation to generation. When Bessie's pain was at its' peak, Granny Mae blew the snuff up her nose. With one big sneeze, Bessie pushed yet another child born out of wedlock into the world.

"It's a boy," Granny Mae announced before handing him to his mother.

Bessie took great care counting each finger and toe, then carefully examined her son's face.

She named my father Leeroy Kinley. He may have had his father's blue eyes, but he bore his mother's maiden name. After three children, John and Bessie were still not married. He gave her a ring, but it wasn't a wedding ring, and she was losing hope that there ever would be.

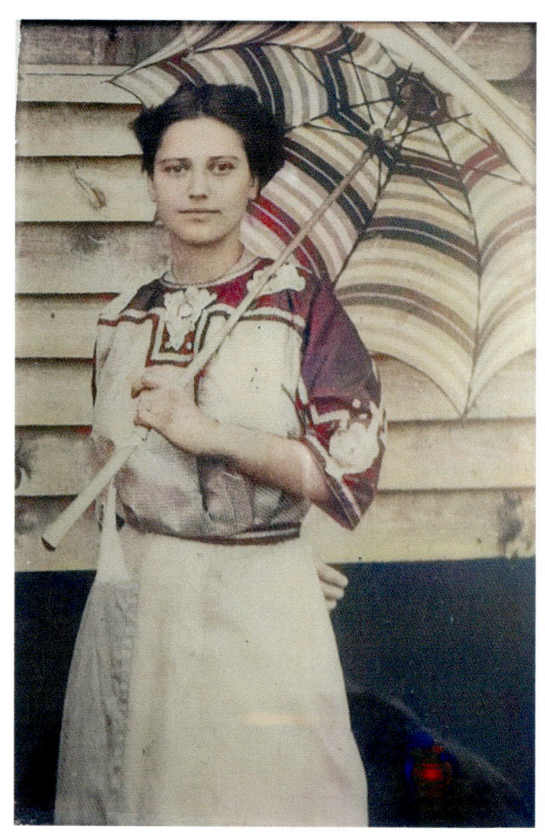

# Chapter 3

*"Over there, over there*
*Send the word, send the word over there*
*That the Yanks are coming, the Yanks are coming,*
*the drums rum-tumming everywhere*

*So prepare, say a prayer*
*Send the word, send the word to beware*
*We'll be over, we're coming over*
*And we won't come back till it's over, over there."*
-George M. Cohan

The winter of 1917 was one of the most severe on record for the eastern United States. North winds blew hard, temperatures dipped low, snow fell deep, and through it all Bessie carried another child. Her fourth pregnancy in four years—another baby boy. He was stillborn.

As spring arrived, World War I raged in Europe. Posters were hung around town encouraging men between 18 and 45 to *do their bit – enlist now*. For the first time in American history the United States prepared to send soldiers in a mass mobilization across the Atlantic to defend foreign soil.

John and his brothers immediately responded to Old Glory's

call to arms. After training as a mounted orderly, then more training at Camp Sevier, South Carolina, the 113th Field Artillery Battery F, and the small-town boy who had never ventured very far outside Concord's city limits, crossed the Atlantic with weapons and tanks to fight for democracy in what they were calling the "War to end all Wars." The Wadsworth home displayed three red stars in their front window for each of their three sons serving overseas.

Back home, parents, wives, and children lost no time busying themselves to do their part to lessen the suffering and hardship of their men overseas. Farmers grew one-acre Victory Gardens. The government urged them to sell their crops to buy War Saving Stamps from children that sold them on street corners.

Germany was not the only enemy the soldiers faced. A strange disease of epidemic proportions began to stalk the soldiers lying in the cramped, dirty, damp trenches of Europe. The troops moving around by ship and train rapidly spread the undetected virus that made its way around the world and became known as the Spanish Flu—the pandemic of 1918.

The epidemic was killing more people than the war. Back home there were two kinds of people—those who were sick with this influenza and those who were trying to save them. Few communities escaped the epidemic and even fewer had resources to care for the sick. Doctors and nurses were serving overseas, so women formed local chapters called *Mothers of War* to care for their wounded boys when they returned home. John's mother Willie was president of the local chapter and lovingly nicknamed "Mother Wadsworth" because of her tireless efforts. John followed reports of the flu back home through letters and newspapers. Many of the soldiers who faced death daily on the front lines also mourned relatives dying an ocean away from the war. Back in Concord, Bessie's father Charlie died that fall.

The sheer volume of soldiers landing in Europe guaranteed an end to the great slaughter and destruction. At the eleventh hour, on the eleventh day, of the eleventh month Germany was not able to replenish its forces. Gradually the machine guns and rifles ceased firing. The cannons quit. The calm was too much. Exhausted men broke and fell where they were. Germany and the Allies agreed to cease fire.

A banner was hung across South Union Street, "Our Boys Are Coming Home – Welcome Back." Local parades greeted the trains carrying hometown heroes, but some soldiers waited months for a seat on a ship to go home. The local newspaper posted casualties and Bessie checked it often. Starting at the bottom moving up to the 'W's. . .Wiggins, White, Wells, Walker . . . No Wadsworth listed. She waited day after day for John's train to arrive.

The boys in the mill resented girls who dated outside the village and the boys who courted them. A mill hand named Will Taylor registered for the war too late to go overseas. While John was in Europe, Will convinced Bessie the Wadsworth heir would never marry her.

Crossing class lines in marriage was taboo. Before John left for the war, he gave Bessie a pearl necklace and a promise, but deep down she knew a boy from uptown would never disrespect that tradition and marry a girl from the mills. Letting go didn't mean giving up, but rather accepting that there were things that could not be.

Bessie was four months pregnant with Will's baby when they said, "I do" at their courthouse wedding. John returned home to civilian life six weeks later. Crowds gathered in the streets around the soldiers anxious to hear their stories about what happened overseas. Bessie was noticeably absent.

Most of the soldiers had never been far from home before the war. The men that returned were much different than when they left, and for John, the life he left behind was much different than the one he came back to.

The neighbors on North Union Street threw lavish parties celebrating the return of their boys, but when John learned Bessie had married and was expecting Will's baby, he found no reason to celebrate.

Poor medical care, poor nutrition, and diseases continued to take lives, especially in the mills where medicine and medical care were lacking. Bessie gave birth to baby Fay, but pneumonia took her soon after her first birthday. Will took off before he realized Bessie was already expecting again, for the sixth time.

A year passed before John married Mary Lafferty. She was the daughter of a doctor and grew up in the same social circle as the Wadsworths, so she earned the full approval of John's parents even though she was divorced and had a five-year-old son just a few weeks older than my dad.

When Bessie learned that John had married, she told her son that his daddy died in a car accident with another woman. There was no car accident. He had not actually died.

It was just the death of their love story.

## Chapter 4

*"I have never let my schooling interfere with my education."*
-Mark Twain

Post-war 1920s was time for a change. For the first time, many average Americans could afford to own cars, radios, and telephones. Radios brought the world closer to home. The Model T Ford became the "family pet of the nation." A used Model T could be purchased for as little as fifty dollars. More cars brought the need for good roads and travel to neighboring towns became easier.

Bessie and her sister Ella packed their bags and left Concord with their sons looking for a fresh start. Bessie gave birth to Evelyn in Waxhaw. Then they moved around like gypsies trying to find a place that might be better than the last. In Mount Holly, they took a house for one day, went in and set up the kitchen, cooked dinner, and slept there. The next day, they packed everything up and left.

"What's the matter? Don't ya like us?" the neighbors yelled out the window as the Kinleys drove away.

The chance of finding work in the mills was greater as a team than by oneself, so Uncle Luke, Aunt Ella, and Grandma Bessie all went together to the Ozark Mill in Gastonia. They stopped at a filling station. Luke went inside and there was Will Taylor. It was more than a few years since they had seen him. He asked about Evelyn so Luke went out to the car to bring her in. When they returned, Will was gone. He had jumped out the bathroom window and took off. He was out of work. I suppose he was afraid Bessie would ask for money he didn't have. That was the last time they saw Will Taylor.

There were no gates or fences to separate the factory where Bessie and Ella worked, from the home where they lived, to the streets where their boys played. From a young age, the kids wandered freely in and out of the mill. Playing crossed over to helping—sweeping the floors, carrying in lunch every day, and while they ate, the women taught their sons the basic skills of their job. Bessie tended the spooling machines, so when the threads broke, she taught her son to go underneath and with his small hands tie the broken ends in knots. The machinery kept running. Clothes and hair easily got caught. Fingers and feet were often crushed.

Their days were paced by the sound of the factory bell. Bessie got up early every morning, still exhausted from the day before. She worked long hours, stretching, leaning, and pulling. The slamming and banging of the machines was deafening, the heat excruciating, and the humidity debilitating.

In her later years, Aunt Evelyn wrote me letters recounting

childhood memories of her brother. They began to paint a picture of the mischievous boy that I had only known as a man.

"The professor whipped children without reason," Aunt Evelyn told me, "and Roy was one of 'em."

School was only mandatory up to age twelve, and they didn't have much to gain enforcing education. Children trapped into the factory life at an early age were less likely to look for work elsewhere.

The mill boss would send word when he needed a couple kids to leave the class and come help in the factory. One day Roy was the first one out of his seat without permission. Professor Hart called him to the front and ordered him to bend over. He yanked out a wooden paddle that hung on the wall behind his desk and swatted hard enough to lift Roy out of his shoes."

Aunt Evelyn said her brother stared the professor square in the eye and asked, "Is that all ya got?"

The vein in the old professor's left temple throbbed.

When Bessie found out, she took her son by the hand and marched him back up to school. She'd go toe-to-toe with the devil if she had to for her children. She stormed into that classroom and right over to the teacher's desk. He rose to his feet. His tall, solid frame towered over Bessie like a mighty oak overshadowing an acorn.

"You beat my boy. Now he don't want to come back here," she told him. "I got a good notion to take out a warrant!" She never backed down from defending her own and my dad never got another beating from the professor.

When Uncle Luke married again he moved out in the country to a dairy farm. Dad wanted to stay with him and go to school with his cousin Ethel. It was spring, and school was almost out, so Bessie let him go. He was beginning to nourish a seed of rebellion. Uncle Luke was one of the few men in his life, and he was needing some male guidance, but Uncle Luke may have not been the best role model. Bessie learned they were all playing hooky, so she made her son come back home. He was only in the sixth grade when he quit school.

Not all the keys to my dad's life unlocked doors of hardship. Some opened wide to fond childhood memories which served as diversions to an otherwise challenging existence. He and his cousin Ruben spent a lot of time romping through the woods in search of the ghostly horseman of King's Mountain, an apparition Grandma Bessie said she saw when she was a child. One day her mother led her with one hand and her brother Luke in the other. They trudged along a dirt road heading to visit Aunt Sallie. In the far-off distance, the silhouette of what appeared to be a man on a horse galloped towards them. He bolted past sending a flurry of dust swirling about. Everything settled, yet something seemed odd. They realized the sound of the horse's hooves beating on the ground could not be heard, nor was there even a trace of the mighty steed's hoof prints left in the dirt. They turned to catch another glimpse, but the horseman mysteriously vanished.

"The legend is," my dad explained as he later led his cousin Ruben down that same dirt road, "a British soldier back at the Revolution was carrying some stolen plans. He was on his way to warn the Brits and stopped at a tavern for rest. He was," my dad looked behind him to be sure no one else could hear, "murdered," he whispered, "by the innkeeper . . .while he slept." Ruben's eyes grew big,

"People say they still see him here on moonlit nights looking for help at this very crossroads." Dad pointed to the ground where they stood. "They say he seems to be confused, and if you try to approach him, he disappears."

"You're makin' this up, ain't ya, Roy?"

"No I ain't . . . shhhh." They stood silent. "Ya hear that?"

Ruben nodded. They got down on their bellies and crawled under the bushes. They couldn't see a thing as they peered through the thicket. They listened. The undeniable sound of a four-beat gait approached. An animal? A large animal? It stopped occasionally and nibbled at the foliage, but kept moving in their direction. Finally, they were so close they could've reached through the bushes and touched him. They both knew this might be their only chance to witness the apparition and didn't want to miss it. In silence, they listened as he came closer—so close they could feel his warm, moist breath as it exhaled across their faces.

Dad moved his lips without giving voice to the question, *Are ya ready?*

Rube nodded his head *yes*. Without any warning, they sprang to their feet, ready to meet the ghostly vision face-to-face. They caught him off guard. His dark black eyes pierced theirs. They all froze in their tracks, standing motionless until Dad's laughter broke loose.

He dropped to his knees and laughed until tears streamed down his face. "It's a donkey! Nothin' but a donkey! And a scroungy one at that! Ya want to take him home?"

Rube remained sullen. "Our mamas won't let us keep a donkey at the house!"

"Well, we won't know if we don't try. Come on, Rube. You need to put on your big boy britches!" His lack of adventure was frustrating. "You can't hide behind your mama's skirt the rest of your life!"

Ruben was still skeptical. "How will we get 'im all the way home?"

"We'll ride 'im!"

"Ride 'im? We don't even have a rope."

"Rube, where there's a will, there's a way! Now come on! Help me find something to catch 'im with."

They searched the woods until they found a long piece of vine, wrapped it around the donkey's neck and climbed up on his back, then rode him down the mountain like a couple of cowboys.

Aunt Ella grinned from ear to ear watching those boys come down the road on that donkey. "Hey, Mama, look what we found!" Rube called out. "Can we keep 'em?"

"We can barely put food on the table as it is," she hollered back without hesitation. "We cain't feed no donkey."

"I told ya they wouldn't let us keep 'im," Ruben whined.

"Who's idear was it?" Aunt Ella looked at both of them and waited for a confession. "I'm gonna wear you both out if ya don't turn around, and take it right back where ya found it."

The boys spent countless days courageously exploring those hills in search of the ghostly vision, but boyhood was quickly vanishing.

The noise inside the mill was a part of my grandmother's life. Thousands of whirring spindles produced a deafening roar that bombarded the workers before they even entered the building. Every conversation while working was a shouting match.

Paydays were spread far apart, so when wages were spent, they had no choice but to shop at the company store on credit. Most employers would simply deduct your bills from your weekly earnings. The cycle of indebtedness ensured workers would stay till the debt was paid back in full. At the end of each month Grandma Bessie and Aunt Ella owed their soul to the company store.

The constant mist from the sprayers on the ceiling in the weave room caused slippery floors. That and the unwholesome habit of chewing tobacco or dipping snuff while tending the fast-moving machinery were partly to blame for hair, clothes, hands and arms getting caught in the belts.

A shuttle once flew off the loom and smashed Uncle Luke's toe. He fell into the spinning machine. One hand went through the gears and crushed his fingers. His wages stopped and there was no money for a doctor.

Once healed, Uncle Luke came back to work in the carding room breathing a fog of dust. He'd cough sometimes until he almost strangled. They called it *Monday morning sickness* because it was always worse after your lungs had a few days off.

By the time my dad was thirteen, the dust from the cotton that silently invaded his lungs, provided a breeding ground for tuberculosis. He waited six months for a bed in the state sanitarium, also known as *death's waiting room.*

The treatment for the fever, coughing, chest pain, and waking up at night drenched in cold sweat was plenty of rest, isolated in the mountains sleeping on an enclosed porch ventilated and filtered by the pungent perfume of the pine trees.

There was an omnipresence of the shadow of death, but the staff tried to brush it off with aphorisms about being strong and determined. Patients were forbidden to talk about their condition with the other patients.

His experience was an encounter with mortality, and Dad returned home from convalescing more determined than ever not to be stuck in the cotton mills, but he wasn't the only one looking for change.

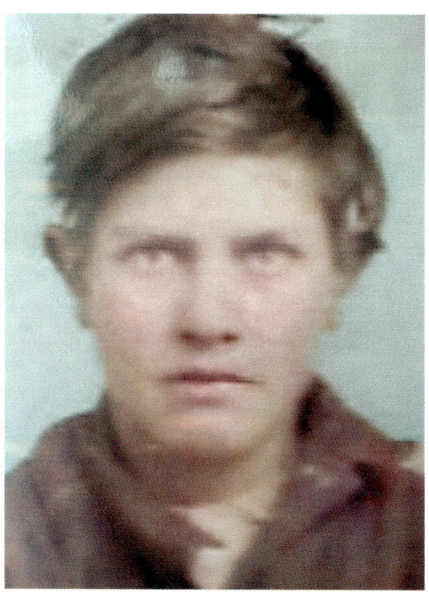

# Chapter 5

> "The lack of money is the root of all evil."
> -Mark Twain

## 1929

While the rest of the country roared through the 20s, the textile mills tightened control over their workers. The "stretch outs" required more work for less pay. Twelve-hour shifts became harried affairs—rushing from one machine to the next under the relentless tick of the clocks.

Union organizers came from up north to fight for a forty-hour work week and at least $20 a week pay. More than anything else, the workers, desperate to put food on their tables, wanted to be heard, but standing up to the boss who owns the houses their workers sleep in and who pay the police to patrol the village wasn't easy in a southern mill town.

The union leaders passed out flyers about a meeting at their makeshift headquarters. The Gazette ran ads to expose them as Red—Bolsheviks, employed by a communist organization, but each night the room filled with the poor, desperate, white labor pool anxious to hear what the strangers from up north had to say. The older ones, born in the mountains, retained some of their pride and independence, but after a generation or two many of the young people were reduced to a sense of inferiority—deprived, destitute, and dependent with bosses who took advantage of them.

Organizers stirred up the crowd. "America is a land of freedom, and opportunity. We believe in this country, and we have the right to organize a union!" The enthusiasm was as contagious as a case of poison ivy.

Bessie and her sister lined up at the table to sign a union card. "We got nothin' to lose and maybe somethin' to gain."

The union organizers granted a voice to the downtrodden, and before long the town's ministers began raising theirs.

"The hand of oppression is growing on our people," one preacher shouted from the pulpit. "In the Old Testament we see how the children of Israel were forced to work for the Egyptian task masters. When they failed to reach their quotas, the whip was cracked across their backs, until Moses rose up and led the first strike. You women are working for practically nothing. They keep giving you less and expecting more. You must come together and insist that such things cease."

Hundreds of workers joined the union. The owners fired a couple of them in hopes of scaring others from following suit. Over a thousand angry workers gathered out near the railroad tracks. They voted to strike.

Over two thousand employees walked out of the mills and paraded triumphantly down Main Street in Gastonia chanting, "We need change! We demand change!"

They carried signs of protest identifying themselves as union sympathizers. Tensions boiled over into violence. Police officers charged into the parade of strikers with fists, bayonets, and rifles. The ones who walked out of the factory were evicted from their mill village. Supervisors threw their belongings out of their homes. The homeless families set up a primitive tent camp on a vacant lot across the street. Scuffles broke out most nights. Prowlers attempted raids on the village and tried to poison their water supply. Restless strikers wanted to carry guns, but the union leaders held them off.

About twenty masked men came to the tent camp late one night. They cut off the electricity, then used hatchets and pickaxes to tear down the union headquarters. One smashed out a front window. The others went in and raided the relief station. They dumped food supplies everywhere, then poured kerosene over it. Some of them were mill bosses. Some of them were lawmen. All of them left with a vengeance. The governor sent in the National Guard and local men were sworn in to stand as armed guards. Caravans of vigilantes cruised the streets.

The smell of danger filled the air, and the odor was pleasant to young boys looking for excitement. Dad watched as Gastonia—the South's City of Spindles, disintegrated into a barroom brawl.

By the end of the month, Bessie could no longer afford not to work. She was forced to return, but many staunch strikers stood their ground.

Violence and the link between the unions and communism

brought negative attention worldwide to Gastonia and the local folks were angry. The tide was beginning to turn, and the number of protestors dropped while their cause wrinkled and grayed.

The defeated workers lined up single file with blank faces and unresponsive eyes and continued working to the rhythm of the factory until October.

News of Black Monday and the crash of the stock market swept the streets of Gastonia and across the country with speed and ferocity that left everyone dazed.

People panicked and ran to withdraw their money. Banks ran out of cash and shut their doors, and many people lost whatever savings they had. Families unable to pay their mortgages lost their homes. Businesses closed, and millions of people became unemployed. Thousands who couldn't find jobs took to the roads, riding the rails to look for work.

Parents were not able to provide their children with necessary books and supplies to attend schools. Taxes, especially in rural areas, went unpaid. With loss of tax revenues, schools struggled to keep operating. Education abandoned three million children. Disease and malnutrition escalated.

Homeless people set up tents and cardboard box shantytowns throughout the nation called "Hoovervilles," as many blamed President Hoover for the way the country was suffering.

The worst drought in history combined with erosion to cause

The Dust Bowl that crippled agriculture in the Midwest shifting thousands of displaced people off their farms as they migrated west.

Back in Gastonia, our dad looked beyond the borders that tried to hem him in. Whether you lived in the city, on a farm, or in the mill village, times were bad.

No one entered the 1930s without being affected by the Great Depression. The American Dream became a nightmare. Despair prevailed.

*"He that waits upon fortune is never sure of a dinner."*
-Benjamin Franklin

I continued to work the puzzle of our father's life gathering pieces from the police station, the courthouse, and the library, but it was over many beautiful telephone conversations with Aunt Evelyn in her later years that her abandoned memories came to life. She carried us back to relive the days of their youth.

"We liked to play jokes on one another," she reminisced. "Roy always hatched stuff up. When the Depression hit, we saw it hard. All the people we knew was stripped of what little they had including their dignity. The more well-to-do families," she remembered, "sold their heirlooms for cash to live on, but in the mill village we didn't have nothin' worth sellin'.

Then radios came along. The music gave us a way to escape the hard times—a connection to the outside world. When the Pritchard family moved in, they brought the first radio to Avon Street. Mama and some others petitioned the boss to start the workday earlier so they could be home in time to listen to Amos and Andy. Ever' evenin' after supper all the families gathered over on the Pritchard's front porch. The men chewed tobacco, and the women gossiped. We all tapped our toes to hillbilly music.

Roy was running with a couple guys and three or four girls at that time. One of 'em was the Pritchard's middle daughter Pauline. She was pretty with black hair, and I know he cared for her, but those boys was no good. Billy Barkley came here from the Stonewall Jackson Reformatory for Boys. Howard Brackett; he even made the preacher want to cuss."

In 1934, another strike took over the streets of textile mills throughout the south. Some said this uprising was the closest thing to a revolution they had seen.

Children who grew up in the mills typically followed in their parents' footsteps generation after generation. Dad was not content to settle for the harsh working conditions and limited opportunities the mill village afforded. He first broke the cycle the Kinley family was stuck in when Carl Bell over at Honey-Kist hired him to deliver ice cream to the dwindling few in Fairmont Park who could still afford it. He also discovered his talent as a landscaper at the big homes on the other side of town.

Observing life on the other side of the tracks inspired Dad's plan to increase his profits by breaking and entering the big homes over in Fairmont Park and selling their stolen goods at the pawn shop. His plan included Billy and Howard. They split the profits and repeated.

That year the Gastonia City Directory shows Roy Kinley living at 210 Avon Street and listed his occupation as "salesman." I had to smile.

## 1993

My sisters and I persevered through rolls of microfilmed newspapers at the Gastonia Library. We tried to kick open the door to our dad's past without knowing exactly what he did or when he did it. Terry and I decided to try the police station.

"No," the clerk at the front counter informed us. "We don't have records that far back. Well, we do," she back pedaled, "but they're in storage in the basement."

Our three pairs of shoes clip clopped in rhythm as she led us down two sets of linoleum stairs through a dark narrow basement hallway into a windowless room with fluorescent lights and the musty odor of old books.

"See . . ." The clerk flipped on the light switch. "It would be like finding a needle in a haystack."

Surveying the sea of black legal-size binders that held archived criminal records in no particular order took the wind right out of our sails.

"I came all the way from California to find out what kind of trouble our dad was in," I explained, "and . . ."

"Here it is!" Terry shouted. "Roy Kinley. He's right here!"

The first book she sifted through contained the very nugget we were panning for.

July, 1934~State vs. Roy Kinley.
Defendant pleads guilty.

The clerk we befriended only twenty minutes earlier joined Terry and me jumping up and down like we just won the lottery and planned to share it with her.

We stood in reverence running our fingers over the page retracing the familiar signature he signed almost sixty years earlier, then we went back to the library with the date he appeared in court. The clerk said, "Back then when you commit a crime you'd be in court right away."

We looked for newspapers on microfilm from just a few days before and found the article.

**The Gastonia Daily Gazette**
Monday Afternoon, July 23, 1934
Youth 19, Admits Daylight Robbery of Spencer Home

Roy Kinley 19, of Avon Street, Gastonia has confessed to the daylight robbery at the home of Mr. and Mrs. W. T. Spencer on South Lee Street in the residential section.

The robbery was committed about 10 o'clock Friday morning, police said. The Kinley boy gained entry to the house which was closed and locked, by cutting a hole in a side, downstairs screen, then breaking a window pane and unlocking a window, which he crawled through. Dense shrubbery about the window hid his actions from neighbors, it was said.

Mr. Spencer discovered the theft when he came home about noon Friday. He immediately notified police. Police Chief Carl Elliott made a thorough inspection of the looted house and took fingerprints from several articles. A short while after Gastonia police had been advised of the robbery, they received a long distance call from Charlotte police, saying they had caught a boy riding the blinds of a passenger train that had come in from Gastonia.

They said he had a valuable watch on him with the initials, "W.T.S." engraved. Local police immediately recognized the watch from this description as Mr. Spencer's watch, which was one of the stolen articles, and ordered the boy held.

He was brought back and after a little questioning confessed to the robbery. He said two other boys were with him, but police were inclined to discredit this theory. He directed police to his home on Avon Street where before leaving for Charlotte, he had hidden the stolen articles, all of which were identified as missing from the Spencer home.

The loot was stashed in a shoe box and consisted of several fountain pens, a bracelet, a pocket knife, several foreign coins, and a vanity case. He told police he had taken one shirt and an old watch. He denied taking several other shirts said to be missing. The table silver could not be located. Kinley denied taking any silver.

Young Kinley waived preliminary hearing and was

bound over to Superior Court. He was held in jail in default of $500 bond.

The Gazette later reported, "Three white boys appeared in court pleading guilty to charges of housebreaking and larceny."

Grandma Bessie and Aunt Ella sat near the front of the courtroom twisting their hankies in nervous anticipation. Evelyn's teacher came to show her support.

"Mr. Kinley, Mr. Brackett, Mr. Barkley," the judge began, "the first time you even thought about a robbery, you planted a seed. The more you thought about it, you nourished that seed and allowed it to grow." He peered over his glasses. "If you continue down this path, you will reap a harvest of bitter fruit. I'm going to sentence each of you to four months of hard labor working on the roads in a chain gang."

He slammed his gavel firmly on the polished oak bench. "For the five years after that, I don't want to see you back in my courtroom again or you'll return to do three more years on the chain gang You'll wish you'd paid attention to my warning!"

The three teens were driven four hours up north into the Blue Ridge Mountains between Virginia and North Carolina, where the road camp in Sparta used convicts in the most brutal form of forced labor in the United States . . . just for stealing a couple fountain pens and some junk jewelry.

# Chapter 7

*"The only real mistake is the one from which we learn nothing."*
-Henry Ford

Chain gangs flourished throughout the South in the 20s and 30s. Convicts chained together, forced to labor at back-breaking tasks such as ditch-digging and road construction were a common site along southern roads. The spectacle of prisoners in chains evoked memories of slavery. Often the pettiness of the crime did not fit the severity of the punishment. The conditions were brutal and shameful, but the labor was free. Bad boys were sentenced to make good roads.

White-tailed deer emerged from the forest to graze on meadow grass at the mountain base. Sunlight and shadows danced across a broad tapestry of stone as the men ascended up the mountain in the back of a cattle truck headed to the unknown. The raw strength of the ragged rocks commanded attention of the imposing view over miles of trees that appeared bluish in color. The road they followed reached a dead end at Camp 16-State Convict Road Force.

"This ain't my first time here," Billy Barkley warned my dad and Howard. "They're gonna move us 'round in a cage like circus animals, 'cept in the circus they only have one or two animals in a cage, not a dozen men! Ya sleep in a stack, five high—one on top of the other, jest a few inches between. You ain't gonna like it!"

Monday morning the rising bell rang at five-thirty, and the guard flung open the door to greet them. "Get up, you lazy SOB's," he yelled. "It's time to get in your cages. We're gonna go out and teach you how to build some roads today."

They lined up single file to have their leg irons put on.

"Well, look at us," Howard turned slowly modeling his new garments. "Stripes—the trademark of all fashionable inmates."

Five of them were chained together. They had to move in rhythm in order to avoid injuring each other. The prisoners that had been there a long time suffered shackle poisoning where the irons ground against their skin. Gangrene and other serious infections set in. With the hobble on, they couldn't walk freely. At best, it was a shuffle—the convict shuffle.

A line formed to leave camp, and the walking boss gave orders. With heavy chains and a broken spirit, they shuffled along accompanied by guards looking anxious for any excuse to fire. One aimed at the line leader, one aimed at the tail end. At all times the prisoners had to be within sight of the guard, but at no time closer than thirty feet to him.

They were loaded into a cage about 8 feet by 24 feet pulled by a mule that transported them to their worksite.

The captain demonstrated how to use a pickaxe. He made it clear, he would only show them once. They split stones while the sun reflected off the surface like little mirrors burning their faces and arms. They moved boulders until their backs ached. They raised the picks over their heads and sank them deep into the hard clay. The smell of earth permeated their nostrils. Perspiration dripped from each face, but the rules didn't allow a brow to be wiped without first getting permission. There were no chainsaws and bulldozers, only axes and shovels. The calluses on their hands dried, cracked, and bled. The days were long, and the work unyielding.

As the noon sun beat down, a voice somewhere along the line began to chant a half-sung phrase. Another voice joined in, and another, until the whole chain gang sang in harmony.

*"Quit cryin'! Quit dyin'! Give dat white man sumpin on your time.*
*I would'a told you, but I thought you knowed. Ain't no heaven on the county road.*
*Six months ain't no sentence, twelve months ain't no time.*
*Done been to the penitentiary doin' ninety nine.*
*Quit cryin'! Quit dyin'! Give dat white man sumpin' on your time."*

The music helped them work in rhythm, but more importantly, it soothed the sorrow of their heavy hearts and brought a peace that transcended and changed, if only for a moment, the miserable conditions of their lives.

In a society committed to segregation, negroes and poor whites shared a solidarity in the chain gangs where they worked side by side from sunup to sundown at gunpoint under whips and chains in a public spectacle. The black men outnumbered the whites two to one and were often treated with greater brutality. A first-time petty thief was treated the same as a murderer.

They worked long hours, six days a week, rain or shine. In the cold weather, the guard dropped a canvas down over the sides of the cage. He threw a bucket of disinfectant down once a month to clean the cage, but that didn't stop the foul stench that permeated.

The first and third Sunday of the month was visiting day. Dad didn't have any visitors, but he sat out in the yard watching the ones who did. There were two barbed wire fences about five feet apart. The convicts stood behind one, the visitors behind the other. Mothers held up their children to get a better look at their daddies. The guards studied their every move. Cars pulled in, and anxious visitors jumped out.

Only once a familiar car pulled in. The door flung open and Evelyn jumped out.

Carl Bell drove her and Bessie up to visit. "Your mother's havin' a hard time without you home, Roy. She needed to come see for herself that you're okay."

"Cousin Eugene died," Evelyn interrupted.

"Eugene? He's only fourteen. What hap?"

"Pneumonia," she answered before he finished. "And Baxter and Myrtle had a baby. A boy. They named him after Uncle Bill, but he only lived two weeks 'fore he died. Mama's takin' it all hard. The sooner you get back, the better."

She shared news from back home until a guard fired a shot in the air to signal visiting time was over.

Bessie watched Howard and Billy across the yard. "I done told ya, those boys you been runnin' with are no good. Ya lay down with dogs, ya get up with fleas. When you get home, I don't want to see them hangin' around anymore."

After four months they released my dad to go home on five-year probation. Determined to walk the straight and narrow and never return, he resolved to distance himself from Howard and Billy. He told himself that he would be smarter, and he was—for a while.

# Chapter 8

*"The spirit of man is more important than mere physical strength."*
-Dwight D. Eisenhower

"I Can Make YOU a New Man, Too,
In Only 15 minutes a Day!"

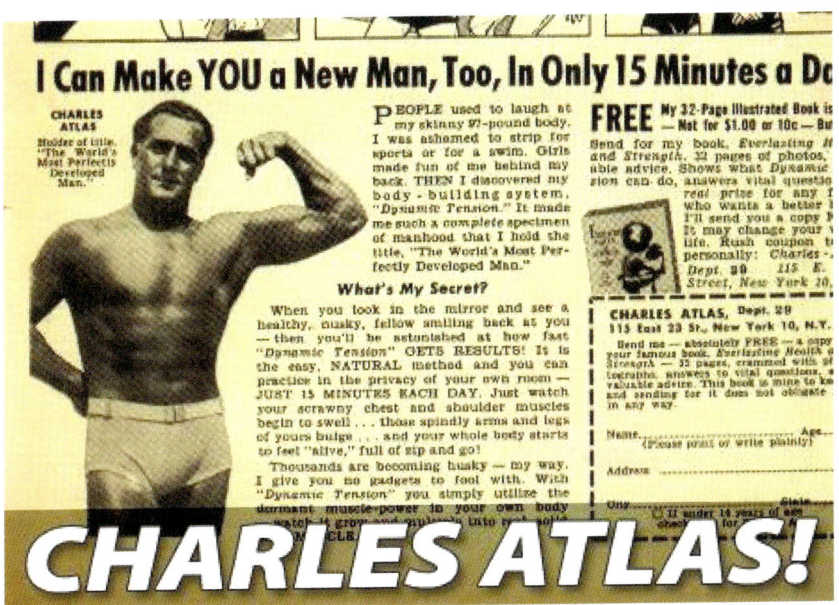

The picture on the back cover of the True Story magazine embodied the ideal of a self-made man—a dream of self-improvement. It went on to read, "A rapid transformation begins with a strengthened healthy body, but also encompasses confidence, ambition, and worldly success."

For $1.98 complete, the ad promised to turn any man into the next Charles Atlas in only six months. Vanity must have gotten the best of my dad. He decided to do it. It took a while to save the money.

When the long-awaited package arrived in the mail, Evelyn raced down the road grinning from ear to ear, screaming, "It came. It came!"

By the time she reached her brother she was out of breath. The expression on her face begged for just a moment to rest.

"Race you home," he dared her showing no mercy.

Dad charged through the front door where the parcel waited on the kitchen table. Evelyn followed close behind, determined to watch him open it. Her eyes were like saucers as she peered into the box. It was small and lightweight. He cautiously revealed the contents.

Evelyn burst into laughter. "I wish I had a picture of the look on yer face! They said 'it'd turn ya from scrawny to brawny!' It ain't nothin' but a jump rope!"

He received twelve lesson booklets and a stretchy band. Dad had a choice to make—admit he had been taken, or use the band to accomplish the task he had purchased it for.

He chose the latter and began jumping rope, increasing his

repetitions daily. He tied one end of the rope on a log, threw the other over a tree branch, and used it like a pulley raising the log up and down. Then he hooked the rope around the heaviest objects he could find and dragged them until he gave out. He used the rope to jump, pull, drag, stretch, and climb. By the end of that year, Evelyn had to admit, her brother had not been taken.

He aimed high and hit the mark. His muscles were well defined. His physical strength was greatly increased, but the hard times decreased his inner strength.

Howard and Billy went back down the muddy path trying to find green meadows. Their names spread through police circles like wildfire in dry weeds. They soon drew Dad back into the fold, and again he chose what seemed to be the easy road to success—scouting out homes where the owners were gone and taking what they wanted. They sold the goods at the pawn shop in Charlotte and spent the cash like there was no tomorrow.

Billy and Howard spent one afternoon loafing at the Southern Railway station in Charlotte. It was a warm place to hide in cold weather and a convenient stopping point for two fareless travelers. Sheriff Krider walked through the station looking for suspects in the robbery of his own home. Howard brushed elbows with the law as he hurried out the door in a hasty retreat. The sheriff looked Billy up one side and down the other taking a close look at the toes of the shoes he was wearing.

"Son, are you wearing low quarters?' the sheriff asked.

"No, sir, these are high-top boots."

"Let me see them." The sheriff pulled up the leg of an overall. "Son, that looks like my boots that was stolen from my home in Salisbury on Tuesday."

"Naw, they aren't neither. I got them from that boy that just passed you going out the door," Billy said.

"Then why do you look as nervous as a long-tailed cat in a roomful of rockin' chairs?" Sheriff Krider grabbed Billy's arm and held him securely to prevent his escape. "Now look here son, my neighbor told me it was two boys that robbed my house."

"You live in Salisbury?" Billy asked naively.

"Listen here fella, don't be a wise guy. My neighbor said one of 'em was a tall drink of water, kinda like that boy that just ran away. The other one was short. 'Bout your size I suspect."

"That couldn't of been me sir. I was at the picture show on Tuesday."

"Well you wasn't at the picture show all day, was ya? Because I don't know how else to explain those boots you're wearin'. Those are my boots."

"Well, I may have been in Salisbury last Tuesday," Billy confessed. "We were knockin' on doors askin' for somethin' to eat, but we didn't get nothin'. We rang the bell at one house and no one was at home, so we went in through the side door."

"You went in the side door and helped yourself to somethin' to eat?"

"We didn't know it was your place, Sheriff."

"Did you know those were my clothes that you walked off with?"

"No, sir."

"Did you know that was my watch you took to the pawn shop and sold for $3?"

"No, sir."

"And what'd ya do with the money?"

"We rode a freight back to Charlotte and went to the picture show."

"The man over at the pawn shop said there was three boys that came in to sell that watch. They all gave bogus names. Did you forget your name son?"

"No, sir. I didn't forget my name."

"Then who's the third boy? Tell the truth now, and shame the devil." Sheriff Krider tightened his grip on Billy. "I'll squeeze the truth out of ya if I have ta."

"Roy Kinley went to the pawn shop with us, but he wasn't at your house Tuesday. He was home sick in bed."

"Well let's go find Roy Kinley and your friend that took off like a scalded dog."

With Billy in tow the sheriff didn't have to go far to find Howard. He stayed at the police station while Billy gave Sheriff Krider directions to Dad's house. Local plainclothes officers caught him selling a bunch of broken up junk jewelry at the pawn shop. They worked rapidly to assemble the maze of evidence to connect him with some, if not all, of a dozen residence robberies.

The newspaper printed a list of articles found stashed in Dad's room and asked residents to come to city hall to identify them. A warrant was sworn out and he was indicted for housebreaking and larceny, for which he could have gotten up to ten years.

Somehow Dad hired local attorney J.L. Hamme to represent him. He was marshaled back into Judge Williams' courtroom where he came face-to-face with Mrs. Thomas Adams. She identified him as the intruder running out her back door as she returned home, then identified her bracelet as the one he sold a jeweler.

"I told ya those boys was no good!" My grandmother had the last word as they led her son out of the courtroom and back into three years of hard labor in chains.

# Chapter 9

*"Sooner or later everyone sits down to a banquet of consequences."*
-Robert Louis Stevenson/Novelist 1800s

Don't be fooled. If you've seen Paul Newman's character in *Cool Hand Luke,* that movie set in the 1960s did not come close to depicting the abuse and mistreatment of the prisoners in the 1930s. Stories circulated of teenage boys who had been whipped to death and prisoners who died in sweatboxes. Two guards in Raleigh were dismissed for chaining prisoners to a door. Four prison officials and a doctor were brought up on felony charges of mutilation after two black convicts lost their feet due to infection. The pervasive stench of sweat mixed with primitive waste disposal overpowered the cramped quarters. Living conditions and unjust treatment by the guards often caused men to snap.

Prisoner deaths were common, but rarely made public until one fugitive from a Georgia chain gang published his memoir. *I Am a Fugitive From a Chain Gang* was released in the early '30s and the movie based on the book was nominated for three Academy Awards. It began to rip the cover off the abuse, but reform came very slowly.

The prison camp at Dallas, North Carolina, was closer to Dad's home than Sparta where he did his time. His punishment was amplified knowing every person driving by observed the men chained together, hard at work, wearing matching wool stripes that were intended to humiliate. They weren't allowed to lift their head to see who it was.

"Wiping it off," an inmate announced.

"Wipe it off," the guard called out granting permission to wipe the sweat from his brow.

The oppressive dictator scrutinized every stroke as the sledgehammer crushed rocks into gravel, and at the end of the day any man who didn't pull his weight could be taken aside and beat with a leather strap.

Some men spent their free time telling exaggerated stories about their crimes and the bum raps they got. Others gambled anything they could get their hands on—a clean shirt, a piece of cornbread smuggled from the kitchen. Some stole things just for the thrill of it.

One little guard with a big attitude carried a grudge for my dad.

"You think the sun comes up just to hear you crow, Kinley?"

He took every opportunity to make Dad's life unbearable.

Holidays always magnify difficult times. Dad's 21st birthday was three days before Christmas. He had nine months down and more than two years to go. I cannot begin to speculate whether it was bravery, foolishness, desperation, or all three that led to him watching for an opportunity to escape.

Dad had not been born with a silver spoon in his mouth; quite the contrary. He had never experienced any of the finer things in life, but while most kids born into the mill village married there and continued the cycle for generations, Dad was determined not to spend one more day in the mill or two more years in the chain gang.

"Kinley, you're gonna be eatin' nothin' but sodie crackers for a long time!" the guard taunted.

Dad stood up and turned to face his opponent. He leaned in close and promised, "Before this week's up, I'll be drinkin' Coca Cola and eatin' Ritz crackers."

## January 14, 1936

Every night, the men dangled their bare feet off the edge of the bunk waiting for the guard to secure their leg irons together. About 10 p.m. one Saturday night in January, Dad and two other inmates saw an opportunity. I wish I knew what their breaking point was and how well thought out their plans were when the trio forced their way out. The rusted barbed wire coiled across the top of the fence dared the men to come any closer. The smell of freedom invited them to take the dare. The prison's security system was a couple of shotguns and two bloodhounds.

The third man was captured before he made good his escape. Dad and Cecil Greene crossed an icy creek barefoot, then quickly parted ways. Desperate to cast off the prison stripes and all they represented, Dad went straight to his cousin Ethel's house for some dry clothes and shoes.

Attempts to escape were common. Most fugitives were found and brought back.

Moonlight glistened off the freshly fallen snow as fourteen-year-old Evelyn collected enough to make snow cream—a North Carolina tradition. She mixed the snow with sugar, milk, and vanilla and stirred it quickly before the snow melted. Bessie and Evelyn were eating the snow cream when headlights lit up the street out front. The sheriff came inside to deliver the news to my grandma that her son had escaped, and they were looking for him. He warned her of the consequences if she tried to hide him or didn't report his whereabouts.

Evelyn was sent to bed, but couldn't sleep. She listened as the relentless barking of hounds refused to give up. It was late when she heard her brother sneak in a back window to say good-bye.

"The sheriff was already here. Mama can't hide you," Evelyn told him.

"I can't stay here, but I won't go back there. I don't know where I'm going, but I've gotta go now." Dad reached for his mother's calloused hands.

"Wait.. . ." She opened the drawer of her bedside table, pulled out a small purse and dumped out some coins. Dad tried to stop her before she dropped them in his pocket. Grandma was small, but she'd fight to death's end if it meant helping one of her own.

"Evelyn, I need you to take care of Mama for me," Dad instructed his sister. "I'll find a way to send for you both when I get settled somewhere safe. Tell Pauline. I don't know where I'm going. I'll send for her too. I don't know if I can write. They might be watching."

Dad leaned in to his mother for a final good-bye. "I've gotta change my name."

He recognized the faint wrinkles that penned heartache onto her face, but they gave no indication of the spirit inside.

She turned his chin back towards her and examined his face like she did when he was young. "You're so handsome—my golden boy." She looked straight into her son's eyes, "You look jest like your daddy. You take the name Wadsworth. It was your daddy's name. It's a name you can be proud of."

The sheriff banged on the door in front. Dad climbed out the window in back.

An approaching train whistle sailed through the air like someone throwing him a life preserver.

# Chapter 10

> *"Even if you're on the right track,*
> *you'll get run over if you just sit there."*
> -Will Rogers

The train track ran right alongside their house on North Rhyne Street. The oncoming headlights signaled Dad to start running. His feet pounded the ground in rhythm with the train as it struck the tracks; faster, faster, faster. The Charles Atlas workout Dad had sent for became worth every penny. A hand reached down. Dad reached up and clung to it thrusting himself up into the freight car into another world—a world of adventure—the unknown. He closed the door of the railcar shutting out the cold air, along with his past, and stepped outside the law, into a place where men live by their wits. He crawled into a dark corner, shivering like a wet dog on a cold night.

He found himself in the company of a dubious-looking character with wild eyebrows who tipped his hat and mimicked a bow as he took a seat on an old wooden crate. The man reached in his frayed pocket, pulled out a crumpled pack of cigarettes and lit one.

The back of trains was a melting pot of men, young and old.

Some had once been prosperous in business but were running from failure or personal problems. Some had known nothing but poverty. There were skilled and unskilled laborers looking for work in other parts of the country and boys escaping boredom. All trying to quench a thirst for moving and stirred by distant opportunities. Many chose the open air to the misery of a factory job. All had the notion that a better life lay somewhere down the track. The only way they could get there was by hopping on trains for a free ride. They were hoboes, and there were a lot of them.

Thinking of my dad as a hobo was a little hard to wrap my head around. Actually, it was very hard to wrap my head around. Growing up, it was a popular Halloween costume, but I now realize the portrayal was offensive. Hoboes are not bums. A hobo wanders and works, a tramp wanders and dreams, and a bum neither wanders nor works. Hoboes wanted to work. Some helped build the railroads they traveled. Accepting charity would hurt their pride.

Wandering and working was a privilege that belonged mostly to able-bodied white men. Transients riding the rails formed a society of their own. Riding the rails was dangerous and illegal. Many lost a leg. Some lost their life. My dad had been hopping on trains for years for short rides to Charlotte or nearby cities. Why walk when you can ride?

There was much to learn. Hoboes rode on top or inside the boxcars on freight trains, or in the blinds between cars on passenger trains. From a distance they looked like a bunch of blackbirds perched on top of a speeding train. Sometimes hundreds of hoboes hopped on a single train.

The railroads hired tenacious guards called "bulls" to make sure the train carried only paying customers. If you were lucky, they just tried to enforce the fare by taking whatever money you had, but they often abused their power and resorted to violence. They could charge you with a crime and lock you up or enforce thirty days' hard labor on the roads—exactly what my dad was trying to run from.

The Piedmont landscape dotted with dreary mill villages sped by. Along the tracks lay a mangled comrade—a casualty of his battle to survive. A false step, or an ill-timed leap and he froze to death.

When the train slowed down, Dad slid open the door of the freight car, jumped out, hit the ground with a hard jolt, then rolled down a steep embankment. His warm breath hit the frosty air billowing up like a cloud leading ahead. A small army of men and boys appeared as if by magic from every part of the train. They escaped into the woods.

Outside the city limits were "hobo jungles"—makeshift campsites hidden by trees and shrubs—a place to wash clothes, have a meal, and spend the night. Broken mirrors hung from tree limbs for the next transient to shave or brush teeth. Dad followed the aroma of smoldering wood to a campfire. Sparks shot out like dancing fireflies lighting up the perimeter of the jungle. A couple men drinking whiskey warmed their hands and swapped tall tales of the road.

An old mattress hidden in the bushes gave protection from the cold and a place for Dad to sleep a few hours. Before daylight, some rowdy jungle buzzards came through the camp trying to pickpocket and intimidate.

Eight railway lines radiated in all directions out of Charlotte. Like a gambler at a roulette wheel, Dad had to place his bet and choose which way to go. He followed the tracks heading north toward Raleigh.

The train's whistle blew, announcing its approach. He couldn't hop the train too close to town. He knew he might get caught. If he tried too far out, the train would have already picked up too much speed. It would be too hard to catch it. He hid behind a shed that belonged to the railroad and waited for the train to start moving, hoping the conductor wouldn't stop to kick him off once it was in motion.

He ran alongside until he grabbed hold and climbed into the blinds, praying once again he wouldn't be seen. Two more guys jumped on after him. A third one tried farther down the track, but didn't make it. He latched on underneath, clinging to the brake rods, fighting the force of the curves as the train picked up speed. The air was cold. The hot cinders tattooed and burned.

The door slammed shut and the train continued along down the track. Dad studied the empty and overtaxed faces. Their heads nodded in rhythm with the motion of the train. He wondered what circumstances brought each of them to that place.

The old man sitting next to him smelled like tobacco and pine tar on a wet dog. His teeth were brown and rotted. His unshaven face masked his dried and weathered skin. For as rough as he appeared on the outside, his mind was still keen, and he possessed a certain astuteness afforded to those whose survival depended on quick wits and resourcefulness. The older, experienced man pointed to a spot on the floor where if they lay flat, they could feel the heat from the hot water tank beneath the boards.

Dad slept about twenty minutes before the old man gave him a kick, reminding him to get up and walk around. It was his turn to lie down. They slept in shifts, for fear of freezing to death if one of them didn't keep watch.

The old steam engine had to make frequent stops to take on water. As the train slowed down, they slid the door open. Dad strained to read the station signs:

## "Welcome to Virginia"

The letters were big and bold. He bowed his head and breathed a sigh of relief as they crossed over the state line. He didn't know what life held for him, but one thing was for sure. He was no longer running from. He was now running to.

# Chapter 11

> *"Do not go where the path may lead. Go instead where there is no path and leave a trail."*
> -Ralph Waldo Emerson

The Depression lingered on while hoboes foraged the countryside for a meal and a place to lay their heads in exchange for doing odd jobs. Some families were sympathetic to those out of work, while others tired of what they considered freeloaders looking for handouts.

Hoboes carried chalk or coal, and made carvings on a fencepost, tree, or gate to give information, directions, and warnings to those that may be coming after them—the hobo's code. A drawing of a cat meant a kind lady lived there. A triangle with hands cautioned the hobo that the person there has a gun, and sharp teeth warned of a vicious dog. The number eighteen was a secret code to others of the brotherhood that there is someone in that house that will feed you.

Halfway between Raleigh and Richmond, a small, weathered sign dangled from a fence post in the distance. Dad strained to see what was written there. The message scratched out on the worn-out wooden sign was not written in code, but instead transcribed in plain

English for all to see. "Hoboes Fed Here."

He entered through the gate, went around to the back porch, and knocked lightly on the back door. The lady of the house usually brought a plate of food to the back porch. This one welcomed him in and prepared him a meal. The warmth that filled the air did not arise just from the wood stove, but also from the kindness of her heart. She understood the need to pull together and lend a helping hand. Dad chopped wood in exchange for his meal and a place to sleep in the shed out back that night.

Constantly looking over his shoulder put a permanent crick in his neck. The smell of fear filled the air with every passing stranger. Sleep eluded him during the dark hours. Daylight met him head on with the challenge of finding work and food.

I'm not sure how much thought went into his destination or how much consideration he gave to which road he took, for that decision was not nearly as important as how he chose to travel down it. I'm not sure exactly how his survival on the road went either. He needed to get out of North Carolina where he was a fugitive, but he couldn't risk riding the rails so long that he would get arrested and find himself returning to finish his sentence on the chain gang.

He hopped another train and rode it all the way to Union Station—the grand gateway to Washington, D.C. The train's vibrations announced their arrival. The hoboes jumped off outside. The paying passengers entered the station where the gilded barrel-vaulted ceiling towered high above the concourse swarming with thousands of people coming and going. Their shoes tapped on the marble floors. Their conversations echoed through the bustling corridors.

Many people left rural areas to move to the city where the government assisted with meal programs and shelters. The country boy jumped off into a city three times the size of Charlotte and was consumed by the energy and excitement created by the commotion.

President Roosevelt stirred the nation over the airwaves when he spoke. "I see one-third of our nation ill-housed, ill-clad, and ill-nourished."

Soup kitchens offering stale bread and watery soup were prevalent. The soup was usually served with a heavy dose of religion. Each night, my dad followed a well-worn path to a spot on a mission floor in a shantytown among middle class folks who had lost their homes. The Communist party tried to recruit the homeless there and convince them that communism would solve the nation's problems.

Temperatures dropped to the lowest recorded that century. Life growing up poor in the cotton mills went from bad to worse as a fugitive without a home that winter.

Before Dad left North Carolina, he had been given his mother's blessing. "Take the name Wadsworth," she told him. "It was your daddy's name. It's a name you can be proud of."

Leroy Kinley became Royal Scott Wadsworth.

Scott? We have no idea where that came from.

Royal? Evelyn always told him he thought too highly of himself. To me, Royal screams confidence in both himself, and in his future.

*New suit, New name, New man*
*Royal Scott Wadsworth*

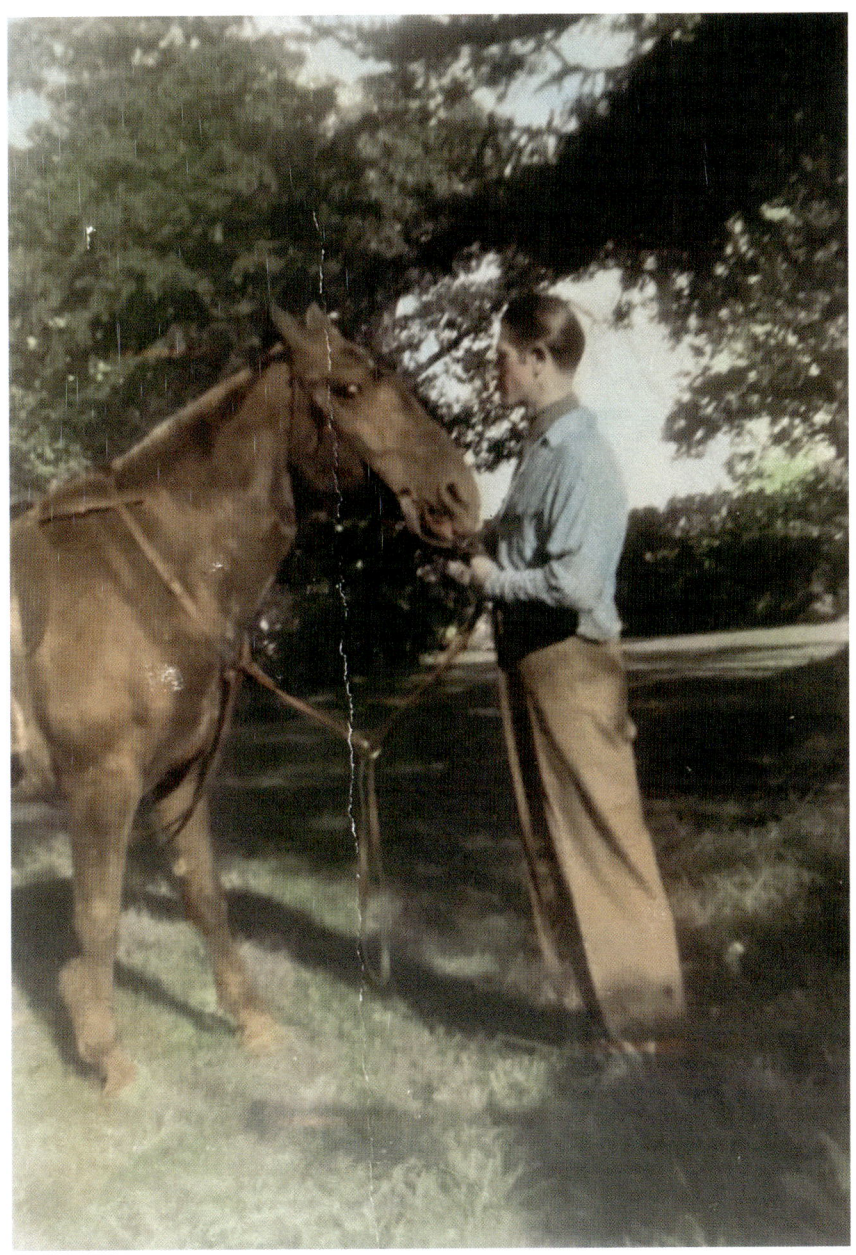

*"I like the dreams of the future, better than the history of the past."*
-Thomas Jefferson

The nickelodeons that showed silent films in the 1920s gave way to luxurious picture palaces with talking movies. It was the Golden Age of Hollywood, and they turned out movie after movie to entertain disheartened audiences.

Popular songs such as "Brother Can You Spare A Dime" spoke to the hardships of the times. Duke Ellington's "It Don't Mean A Thing If You Ain't Got That Swing" summed up the music of the 30s. Big Bands played upbeat tunes, and young people danced their blues away.

Interest in spectator sports grew, and horse racing was legal in twenty-one states. Gambling increased as people looked for new ways to make quick money. The radio at Tom's Lunch Café tuned into George Burns and Gracie Allen's radio show. From the barbershop, Silver's hooves clippity-clopped as they pounded the ground carrying the Lone Ranger in hot pursuit of outlaws. *Jack Benny* provided comic relief to families gathered around their new television set, while the heroics of *Jack Armstrong, All American Boy* thrilled listeners young and old.

Dad blended into society as Royal Wadsworth—just another average Joe, desperately trying to find a job. One in every four Americans was seeking employment. Unfortunately, he was still the one looking, but for the first time in a long while, Dad was filled with optimism as he explored the streets of Washington, D.C.

Once he got settled, he planned to send for his mother, his sister, Evelyn, and even his girlfriend, Pauline, if she was still waiting. Evelyn said he snuck back home one time to let them know he was okay. He rode the train this time as a paying customer, but the risk of being back in Gastonia was great and when he left that time, the letters stopped. Bessie waited and feared the worst.

Country Kitchen was a small diner right down the street from the White House. The owner, Mr. Winsel's wife was fooling around on him. When the troubles at home showed up at work, Mr. Winsel needed help so he told Dad to get a Social Security card and hired him. Before the computer age, no one questioned whatever you wrote on the application. Officially becoming Royal Scott Wadsworth was not that difficult.

A sweet lady named Mrs. Simms ran a clean boardinghouse near the restaurant. She recited a lengthy list of house rules, but asked very few questions and only required one week's rent up front.

Every new beginning comes from some other beginning's end. A new name, new work, and a new home in a new place, but talk about hiding in plain sight! A fugitive from the law gets a job and takes up residence right down the street from the nation's capitol?!

*Dad & Mrs. Simms*

# Chapter 13

*"For truth is always strange; stranger than fiction."*
-Lord Byron

## 1993

Donna, Terry, and I sat three in a row on Aunt Evelyn's sofa ready to discuss the reason for our visit. A hand-crocheted doily carefully placed over the lampshade created a dimly lit living room. Aunt Evelyn carried in an old box from out of the closet, set it on the table, and methodically lifted out its contents—some dog-eared photographs and a stack of brittle, yellowed newspaper clippings . . . family secrets resurrected from their shallow grave. We were still reeling from the news that our dad had a past, when she locked eyes and confessed, "Y'all know we come from a long line of thieves and murderers, don't ya?"

She had pre-made a folder for each of us girls with copies of the tattered newspaper and magazine articles she was about to share. "Mama and Aunt Eller went to their older sister, Sallies' home in Concord almost every Sunday for dinner," Aunt Evelyn told us. While Grandma Bessie worried about when or if she would see her own son again, Aunt Sallie's son, Cousin Baxter, made headlines in newspapers and magazines across the country. Dad may have seen it on the newsstand even in D.C. . . . *Murder Under the Carolina Moon.*

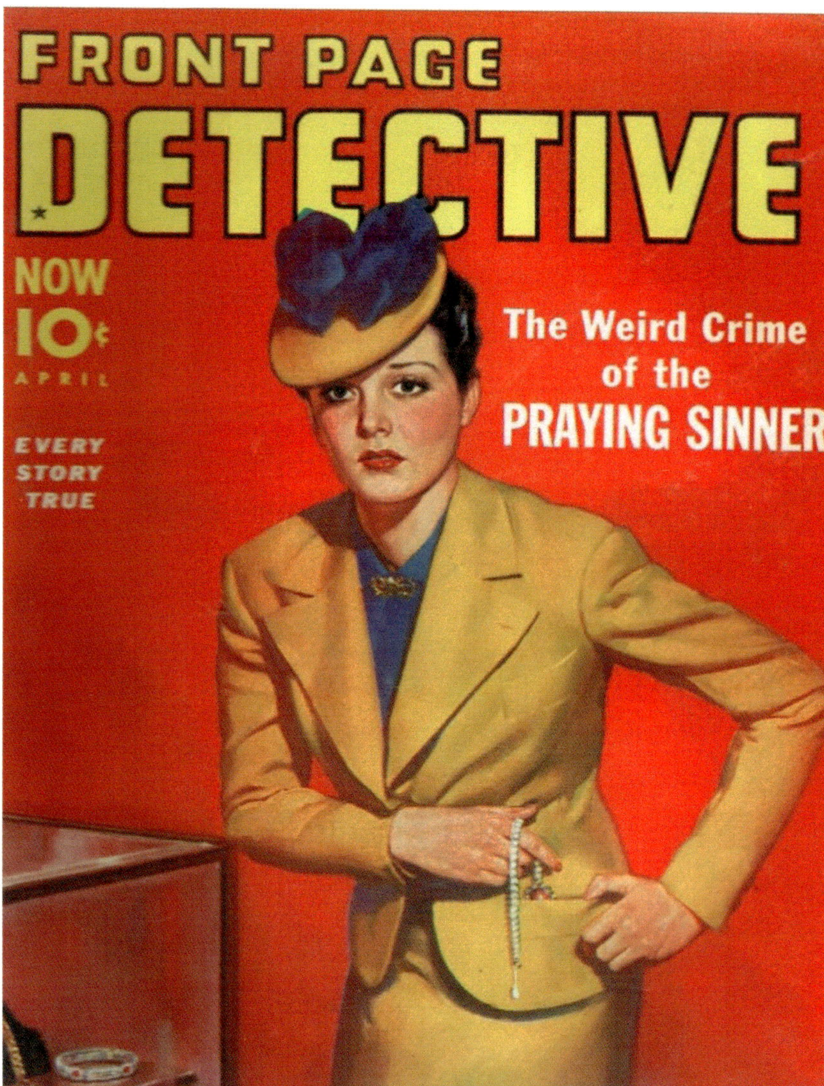

# 1938

Out near Hickory Grove at old Charlie Caldwell's farm lived an older black woman by the name of Jennie Morris who professed she could tell the future. She alleged that as a young girl she was awakened one night from her sleep and beheld a vision of a white and shining spirit who lifted her out of bed, carried her deep into the Carolina tangle woods, and endowed her with powers to heal, and see into the future.

She claimed, "It's a sweet, pretty spirit, with no harm for nobody."

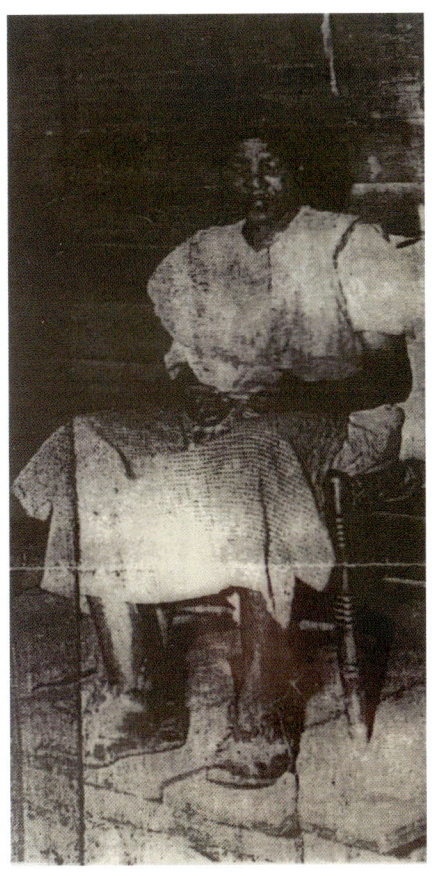

Folks in town called her Aunt Jennie. Most said she was nothing but a witch and didn't want to have anything to do with her, but the deep ruts forged by the many cars traveling down the twisted trail that led to Jennie's house told a different story.

One hot and humid summer evening, cousin Baxter made his way out to the tumbledown shack hidden in the woods and let himself in. The old fortuneteller appeared unmindful of his entrance. The glow from the fire unveiled the dismal surroundings.

There, next to the blackened fireplace, sat Jennie practicing her black magic, rocking to and fro, chanting in a rhythmic beat, "A very good time on hand, a very good time on hand."

"The ol' man won't go 'way," Baxter ranted. "I keep tellin' 'em, 'Leave me alone, ol' man.' He won't go 'way. He's watchin' everything I do." Straining his eyes as if he could see someone, Baxter swung a punch and almost toppled over as his fist met no resistance. "There he is! See'm?" Nervously he ran his fingers through his hair, rambling on in fragmented sentences that made no sense. "He's with that woman. The one with eyes like a cat. I know she can make it all right, if he'd jest go 'way." The more he talked, the more troubled he became. "I see'm everywhere. He's an ordinary man with dark brown hair and a little mustache. Go 'way, ol' man."

Baxter paced back and forth like a wild cat confined to a cage. "People say you got ways to make 'm go 'way. You gotta help me!" he pleaded.

She assured her distraught visitor she could help.

In the shadowy corners of the room, Jenny kept containers of various herbs and charms. Reaching for a small tin from the shelf, she soberly extracted a pinch of the mixture stored inside. "Be careful," she warned. "Be careful 'n rub this 'tween yer hands."

Feverishly, Baxter removed a handkerchief from his back pocket and wiped the sweat from his brow.

"It'll bring ya luck and break the spell that's been cast upon ya."

He did exactly as she instructed but saw no benefit. The following Sunday he made a second visit. This time she reached into a different tin filled with strange-looking roots.

Her dusky eyes drew close to his as she gravely cautioned him, "Don't go inta nobody's house 'til after ya done chewed these roots. Now do as I say," she urged.

He paid her twenty cents. She returned a dime.

By sundown of that evening, he returned home to the farm where he lived with his wife Myrtle, her sister Martha Jane, and his in-laws. His wife was already in bed but still awake.

"Myrtle," he called softly, "why ya in bed? I ain't never seen ya go to sleep this early. What's the matter with ya?"

He found his answer in the tone of her voice. "I was feelin' sick, Baxter," she sulked. "My head's apoundin'. I jest needed to rest."

"You ain't listenin' to no crazy rumors that's circulatin' are ya?"

She replied, "No," but was unconvincing.

"Honey, people's been saying things 'bout me and Martha Jane that jest ain't true." He tried to approach her, but she was cold and distant. "She's yer sister, Myrtle. You know I wouldn't be untrue to ya with yer own sister."

Myrtle sat up in bed. "I want to believe ya, Baxter. Maybe me, you, and Martha Jane jest need to pray fer the whole misunderstanding."

At first Baxter hesitated, but then agreed to his wife's wishes. Myrtle arose abruptly and went to find her sister. Their father had visitors that night, so the three decided to go out back where they would not be disturbed. Stepping out into the twilight, Martha Jane immediately took notice of the full moon.

A chill shivered up her spine. "Full moons cause people to lose their wits," she muttered.

The brush birds ceased their serenade as Martha Jane led them past a field of cotton buds, down toward the barn. Myrtle, trailing closely behind, glanced over her shoulder. Baxter headed back toward the house, grumbling he forgot something.

Thunder rumbled in the distance. Bolts of lightning stabbed the sky. Baxter reappeared, agitated at the sight of the girls behind the hog pen already kneeling with heads bowed, eyes closed. The wind broke loose like a tethered horse running wild. Baxter circled them like a ring of fire. His rage began to smolder.

"I ain't never seen'm like this before," Myrtle whispered. Martha Jane looked up. "Baxter," Myrtle snapped, "kneel down here," but he continued to lap up the voices in his head like a thirsty dog.

"Cat-eyed woman," he hissed at Martha Jane.

Myrtle looked up a second time, irritated at her husband's apparent lack of response to her request. His massive frame towered over them and cloaked Myrtle's face in darkness. As the girls raised their voices toward heaven, Baxter reached inside his overalls, pulled out an ice pick, and raised it over his head, then without hesitation, plunged it into Martha Jane's beating heart.

Afraid she was next, Myrtle curled up like a baby in her mother's womb. "Don't stab me, Baxter! Please don't hurt me!"

The shrill cries of frightened pigs pierced the night like an unwelcome intruder. Exasperated, Baxter kicked the gate to quiet their high-pitched squealing.

Laboring for each breath, Martha Jane fought for strength to stand to her feet. She staggered toward the house. The moan she bellowed brought her father, Israel, running.

"Daaa. . ." she groaned. "Bax. . ."

With one final step, she collapsed into her father's arms.

"Martha Jane! What happened?" Israel's heart pounded like a torrent of rain beating the ground. "Baxter? Was it Baxter?" He swept Martha Jane up and ran as fast as he could. Her blood-soaked blouse dripped a trail leading to his truck. He felt the life draining from her weakened form. Gently laying her frail body on the seat, he took a moment to stroke her golden hair.

"I got ya now, baby girl. Daddy's got ya now."

He sped down the driveway trying to make sense of what just happened. Time was not on his side. As the car rounded the curve, the headlights lit up Myrtle's face. She was frantic—hollering to someone. Israel watched through his rearview mirror as Myrtle clung to Baxter in desperation while he pulled her arms from around his neck, pushed her aside, and took off; flying like a bird trying to escape the trapper. A moan from Martha Jane brought Israel's attention back where it needed to be—the road to the doctor in Harrisburg.

Thrusting down the accelerator, he pleaded, "Hold on, baby. Jest a few more miles!"

The drive seemed to take an eternity, and somewhere along the winding road Martha Jane entered in. Upon arrival at the doctor's house, his little girl lay motionless in a pool of blood. Israel tenderly lifted her head and held it against his chest. Overcome with anguish, he began to weep. He cried out to God, but heard only deafening silence. Tears fell from his face. He watched them trickle down Martha Jane's arm, making their journey's end into the palm of her delicate hand.

Israel took his calloused fingers and gently clasped hers, curling them tightly and folding them shut, then whispered in her ear, "You carry these tears to heaven and give 'em to God."

Baxter ran from the farm toward Rocky River. His mind raced as fast as his feet. He couldn't think straight and wasn't sure which way to go. Gaining speed with every stride, the adrenaline pumped through his veins. The sweltering July night provoked beads of perspiration that stung his eyes. He ran without stopping for two miles until he reached the Rocky River Presbyterian Church. If anyone could help him now, it would be Reverend Ricks, but Baxter had to wait for him to conclude his Sunday evening services before they would be able to talk.

Inside devoutly sweet voices sang a familiar hymn.

> "Some glad morning when this life is o'er, I'll fly away.
> To a home on God's celestial shore, I'll fly away.
> I'll fly away O Lordy, I'll fly away.
> When I die, Hallelujah by and by, I'll fly away."

Outside, the voices in Baxter's mind taunted him. The pastor closed in prayer. The organist continued to play while the congregation dispersed. Baxter burst through the door and rushed to the pulpit hysterically confessing what had transpired back home.

"Calm down, Baxter. I can't understand a word you're saying. You sit here, and wait while I go see for myself."

Arriving at the Finks' farm, Reverend Ricks found the family inconsolable over the loss of their youngest child. He immediately returned to the church and persuaded Baxter to turn himself in at the Concord County jail.

"What's this in yer back pocket?" Sheriff Hoover questioned. "Looks to me like some kinda herb. . . Lespedeza or somethin'."

"I went to see that old negro witch out at Charlie Caldwell's," Baxter explained. "She give it to me. Told me to rub it 'tween my hands and it'd bring me good luck. Then she give me some rattle tongue root to chew to lift me outa my misery. I chewed 'em like she said, then threw 'em in the field."

The cell doors clanged shut behind him. Baxter collapsed on his bunk. He talked freely to the other inmates about the murder, but offered no explanation except that he went crazy from the roots Jennie gave him to chew.

Sheriff Hoover, Deputy Ball, and Coroner Mitchell drove to Israel Fink's farm in the rural county of Cabarrus. Myrtle reenacted what had taken place the previous night. Several feet from where Martha Jane collapsed, they found a blunt, handmade ice pick stained with blood in the bushes. Israel was asked to identify the last

thing that touched his daughter's heart.

The trio then drove to Mecklenburg County, deep into the shadowed grove to the shanty occupied by Jennie Morris. The officers did not identify themselves, but asked to have their fortunes told.

"You's a good little man," she flattered Coroner Mitchell. Then recoiling like a rattlesnake, she struck out at Deputy Ball. "The cards tell me you's the meanest man in this county!"

The officers questioned her at length.

Sheriff Hoover relayed the allegation. "Mr. Parnell tells us that you give him some roots to chew, and while under their influence, he killed his sister-in-law."

Aunt Jennie was disturbed by the accusation. "He came here, all right, but he was wrong in the head. He talked crazy talk. Sed he was mad at some old man. He talked to 'm, but I couldn't see nothin'. I could see my spirits, but I couldn't see no old man. He kept cryin', go 'way! Go 'way, old man!' but I couldn't see 'm. Sed some cat-eyed woman'd make it all right, if it jest weren't for that old man. I got roots to make a salve that helps folk with their misery," she admitted, "but I wouldn't give dat crazy white man nothin'. I was sceared of him."

Jennie entered into a state of seclusion and appeared to be in some kind of a trance. Gazing at her tarot cards, she began to taunt, "I can see him now. That man's in a tight place. He wants to run." Her head fell back and her gray eyes glazed over. "He wants to jest get out and run and run and run."

The courtroom filled to capacity with onlookers anxious to hear every detail of the mysterious hex murder. Paper fans fluttered like hummingbird wings as those in attendance tried to get relief from the hot August temperatures. The overflow spilled out onto the courthouse lawn—the largest attendance at a trial in that county. Bessie came to show support to her sister. Most people in Concord took off work to be there. It's likely that John attended, too.

The bailiff called the room to order. "The state of North Carolina versus Baxter Parnell. Court is now in session."

Israel Fink took the stand first. He laid his hand upon the tattered Bible and swore to tell the truth. Blinded by his tears, he relived the details of that ominous night. Then he turned to the jury. "I been watchin' my son-in-law fer months now. I knew he was jealous of Martha Jane seein' Lewis Furr. I didn't know how long it'd take 'fore Myrtle saw it herself. I took 'm aside and told 'm straight out to stay away from Martha Jane."

The courtroom buzzed like a swarm of flies on a dead carcass as the next witness was called. Old Jennie sauntered down the aisle to testify. She wore a man's hat perched stiffly on her head. The once-shiny black taffeta dress held together in front with safety pins was no doubt her Sunday best. Her stretched-out nylon hose pooled around her ankles and she swam in shoes that were too big.

The prosecutor interrogated her about her potions.

"There's so many. I ain't got time to tell ya," she mocked.

Muffled laughter swept the courtroom.

"Order in the court," demanded Judge Armstrong.

"My potions cure miseries and bring people good luck." Her insidious eyes carefully scanned the courtroom, and all who were present feared they would come to rest on them as she proposed why people sought her out. "Some people come to me fer love charms, and some come to have me throw their babies. Some come fer herbs and lotions to rub on yer hands to bring happiness and peace of mind. Some come fer evil." Jennie continued to probe the courtroom. "I have nothin' to do with them seekin' to do evil."

The people sat spellbound.

Fixing her eyes on Baxter, she denied, "Don't matter what he says. I have no roots to give people to make 'em kill. Specially dat crazy white man!"

"Do you really think Mr. Parnell is crazy?"

"Lawdy, yes, he's crazy." The ragged old woman concluded her testimony and sauntered back down the aisle.

Uneasiness pervaded the courtroom, but none felt it more than Myrtle Parnell. She fidgeted in her seat until the court clerk

summoned her by name. As she made her way to the witness stand, Baxter fumbled in his pocket for something. Knowing he carried a picture of Martha Jane in his wallet, she trembled at the thought of him revealing it there. Unable to hold up any longer under the stress, Myrtle collapsed. Baxter pulled out a pack of cigarettes and tapped them on the table, oblivious of his wife's fragile state. Connie Fink jumped to her feet attempting to rush to her daughter's side. Judge Armstrong promptly warned her to stay back.

"Look at Baxter," Connie whispered in Israel's ear as she took her seat. "He's tryin' his darnedest to intimidate Myrtle so she'll be too scared to testify."

After a full day of testimonies, Judge Armstrong adjourned court for the day.

A reporter from the Tribune rushed to Baxter. "How do you feel the trial's going so far, Mr. Parnell? What did you think when your wife collapsed? Were you worried?"

Ignoring the questions posed to him, Baxter pointed out the reporter from the Charlotte Observer, Bugs Barringer. "He's a liar, and I'm mad at him!" Baxter shouted. "He told me if I let him take my picture, he'd send me a copy of the paper. Said I'd be right there on the front page, but he never sent it. If I'd known he was gonna lie, I wouldn't have never let him take my picture!"

The next morning, the trial resumed with Baxter himself taking the stand.

Baxter's attorney, James Furman, began, "Mr. Parnell, where are you employed?"

"I work fer my father-in-law, sir, Mr. Israel Fink. I worked in the cotton mill fer awhile when I first quit school. Then my father-in-law needed help on his farm, so I left the mill and went to work fer him."

"And Mr. Parnell, where do you live?"

"I live with my father-in-law, sir, Mr. Israel Fink. I moved in there after I went to work on his farm. After a spell I asked his daughter Myrtle to be my wife."

"Jennie Morris told the court that she believes you're crazy." Mr. Furman paused momentarily allowing time for Baxter to refute the statement. "Has anyone else ever told you you're crazy?"

Baxter sat quiet for a few moments before he spoke. "I had a head abscess when I was young. I never got past the first grade. I was fifteen when I finally quit tryin'." He continued to ponder the question. "Once I was injured in my head by an explosion." He looked to the front row where his mother sat painfully listening to each word. "Mama says I ain't got the sense God gave a goose."

"Baxter can you tell me what happened on Christmas Day ten years ago?"

"I tried to emasculate myself."

The rustling in the courtroom withered and fell like leaves.

"I went to the sheriff with my legs and clothes all covered in blood. I told'm a couple of strangers attacked me while I was huntin'. Accused' me of bein' too intimate with some neighbor girls and tried to emasculate me with a pocketknife. The sheriff rushed me over to the hospital. Had me examined by a doctor. Then he took me out in the woods to show'm where I was when it happened. After a couple days, I finally told'm I'd done it to myself to make my girl jealous. A lot a folks sed I was crazy then." Baxter looked at his shoes and played with the laces unaware the jury was beginning to connect the dots.

The prosecuting attorney interrogated Baxter at length trying to throw him off track, but he stuck to his story, not swerving an inch off-course.

"After I chewed them roots, my mind commenced a swimmin'. I told Myrtle and Martha Jane, 'we need to go out in the yard and pray.' My mind kept comin' and goin'. Next thing I remember, Myrtle was shakin' me. I saw blood all over my hands. I knew somethin' was terribly wrong!"

Twelve witnesses petitioned the court, and the jury heard them all.

The prosecutor ended with a final argument. "Martha Jane Fink was loved by people all around for her beauty and kindness. At only nineteen, her life had barely just begun. Baxter Parnell diabolically plotted her death, because if he couldn't have her, no one else could have her either."

Attention then turned toward Baxter as he entered his plea of insanity.

The jurors deliberated six hours before they returned the verdict late Friday night.

The old courtroom on South Union Street was standing room only. The judge ordered Baxter to stand and face the jury. After two months in jail, he appeared a ghost of his former self. His sunken eyes were a direct result of his harassed mind and sleepless nights. He wore a striped shirt with the sleeves rolled up, suspenders, and an ill-fitting necktie. Attempting to smooth his black tousled hair made it apparent to onlookers his appearance was more important than the verdict. While the jurors agreed Baxter was eccentric, they refused to believe the confessed killer was insane.

The judgment was pronounced. "Guilty of murder in the first degree with no recommendation of mercy."

The ruddy-faced Rocky River farmer stood despondent.

"William Baxter Parnell, in accordance with your conviction for the killing of Martha Jane Fink," Judge Armstrong stated, "this court imposes upon you the penalty of death. In accordance with that sentence, it is ordered that you be taken to the state prison in Raleigh, North Carolina, where you shall suffer death by asphyxiation of lethal gas in the facilities maintained by this state for judicial execution."

Baxter turned to face his family drained of all emotion. He hid his face from the flash of the photographer's camera as he was shackled and handcuffed. The crowd filed out of the courtroom. Baxter's mother and his mother-in-law came face-to-face for one brief moment. Though no words were spoken, they communicated in the universal language of motherhood.

Baxter was moved to Raleigh's Central Prison to wait on death row. Mr. Furman worked to appeal his case. The appeals were all denied.

Chaplain Cooper delivered the news. "Baxter," he paused, "Governor Hoey has declined to intervene. Your execution's set for Friday." For the first time, Baxter looked remorseful, but the chaplain wasn't sure if it was because of what lay behind him, or what lay before him. "Is there anything ya'd like to say to clear yer conscience?"

Baxter nodded. "There is, sir."

The two men sat down at a table across from each other with a guard posted nearby.

"There is somethin' I have to say." Baxter swallowed hard. "Out'a fear I give the story about the roots makin' me kill Martha Jane. The fact is," he confessed, "it was more like a fit of anger." His massive fist clinched tightly and pounded the table. "I was sorry right away. You gotta believe me. I even prayed for her recovery, but when I heard she was dead, I got scared."

The chaplain listened intently.

"I did go see that old colored woman. She mumbled some advice and give me some of her magic herbs, but Martha Jane's daddy was right. I'd got myself all worked up 'bout her havin' that new boyfriend. He was comin' to call on her most ever' evenin'. I knew he wasn't right fer her, but she wouldn't listen. I guess it weren't none of my business who Martha Jane give her affection to." Baxter squirmed in his chair, unable to get comfortable. "I take the full blame on myself. I shoulda been honest from the beginnin'. Once the trial started, I thought it best not to change my story. Can you get word to Jennie Morris fer me? Tell her. . ." Baxter dropped his head in shame, "Tell her I'm sorry. Ask her to fergive me."

Chaplain Cooper patted him on the back and reassured him. "I'll tell her."

The thief that robbed Baxter's mind of peace was caught with his confession.

"Do you feel ready to face your own death, Baxter?"

"I feel the good Lord's fergiven me of this terrible thing I've done. My deepest regret is that I'm responsible for plungin' poor Martha Jane into eternity without a moment's preparation."

On December 9, 1938, Baxter was led to his death. Outside the prison gates, Israel Fink stood shrouded in the grayness of a cold winter day within sight of the witness room. Inside, nineteen people gathered to watch as Baxter was led into the small death chamber.

"Good-bye, Chaplain. Good-bye, Warden Wilson. I want to thank you for being so good to me since I've been here."

The chamber was sealed. Baxter's lips moved as though he was saying his final prayer, or maybe singing the hymn that took on new meaning the night he killed Martha Jane.

*When the shadows of this life have gone, I'll fly away.*
*Like a bird from prison bars has flown, I'll fly away.*
*I'll fly away O Lordy, I'll fly away.*
*When I die, Hallelujah by and by, I'll fly away.*

The warden pulled the gas switch. Baxter breathed in the fumes, then surged up in his chair, straining against the straps. His flesh pulled taut against his muscles.

*Just a few more weary days and then, I'll fly away.*
*To a land where joy shall never end, I'll fly . . .*

At a time when newspapers were a lifeline to the outside world, Cousin Baxter's story made international headlines because of his witchcraft defense.

*Kills Woman-Religion Mad* ~ Burlington, NC July 4, 1938
*Ice Pick Hex Slayer on Trial in Cabarrus* ~ Front Page Gastonia Gazette August 25, 1938
*Blames "Witch"* ~ Front Page NY Times August 1938
*Hexed Farmer Is Guilty of Slaying and Must Die* ~ Charleston Gazette, Charleston, VA.
*Farmer Gets Chair For Murder* ~ Wisconsin State Journal August 27, 1938
*Witch Doctor Killing Guilty* ~ NW Arkansas Times
*Jury Dooms Farmer in 'Witchcraft' Death* ~ Salt Lake Tribune August 27, 1938
*Witchcraft Killer* ~ Winnepeg Free Press August 29, 1938
*Curse of Black Magic Is Again In The Land* ~ Nebraska State Journal November 16, 1938
*Slayer Enters Insanity Plea* ~ Reno Gazette
*'Hex' Slayer Put To Death* ~ Burlington Daily Times December 9, 1938
*I Saw My Sister Murdered* ~True Detective Magazine September 1939
*The Weird Crime of the Praying Sinner* ~ Front Page Detective Magazine

Blame it on the Roots-America Bewitched:
The Story of Witchcraft After Salem
Pg. 33

## Chapter 14

> *"Try not to become a man of success, but rather try to become a man of value."*
> -Albert Einstein

1940 was a great time to be an American. The Depression was over, and optimism flourished. Big bands belted out sassy swing in dance halls. Cars had curves. They were built of real metal, and gas was cheap. Cigarettes and red meat weren't bad for you.

Fashion was in a golden age. Even everyday clothes made people look good. Women wore high heels and nylons, and their legs were objects of men's fond reverence.

Americans worked hard. Families were close-knit, manners mattered, and faith was important. America had challenges yet to face, but none seemed too great for a country that was definitely on the upswing.

People's lives had begun to change course. My dad's was no exception. His boss, Mr. Winsel, rewarded hard work, gave encouragement to think big, and instilled in Dad a desire to someday own his own business. He encouraged him to take classes at George Washington Night School. Then, he promoted him to manager at The Country Kitchen.

The icing on the cake was the day my mother, Dolores first

walked into the diner. She had just moved to D.C. with her family from St. Louis and needed a job. Mr. Winsel needed another waitress and hired her immediately. Her thick brunette hair bounced up and down as she waltzed from table to table taking orders. Her emerald-green eyes often caught Dad watching her from the kitchen. He found himself becoming protective of her. When she spent too much time with gentlemen customers, he would pull her away and re-assign that table to the other waitress.

After hours, Willie, the busboy, would drop a nickel in the juke box while he swept the floor, and danced with the broom. The Tommy Dorsey Orchestra played while Frank Sinatra crooned his new hit song, "Dolores".

Even if he didn't believe in love at first sight, the sight of this girl made him believe in love for the first time. Many nights, he lay in bed listening to the radio. Contrary to Mrs. Simms' no smoking rule, he'd sneak a cigarette and spend a lot of time thinking about the kind of girl he'd like to marry. Sinatra's song replayed in his mind.

He asked her out.

She said, "Yes."

Mom later told us she was used to walking or taking the streetcar. He impressed her each time he hailed a cab to get around town.

"How come you haven't told me anything about your family?" she eventually asked, catching him off guard. "Where do your parents live?"

He worried if she knew the truth about his past, she may not have anything to do with him.

"My folks are dead," he fabricated.

Though he felt ashamed to be lying about such a thing, she was sympathetic and didn't ask for any further explanation. He didn't offer any. The chains that bound him had been pried off, but he was still shackled to fear of his past catching up to his present.

Mom dreaded bringing him home to meet her family in fear her father's drinking would be an embarrassment. Grandpa Glen often started drinking Friday nights, faking a story about going hunting and not return home until late Sunday.

He earned a decent wage as a bricklayer, but spent it all drinking and womanizing. Once he left with another woman and told Grandma Mamie to put the girls in an orphanage.

"Don't you even care if you ever see your girls again?" she asked him.

"They can look me up when they get older if they want to," he answered.

The girls both quit school and worked from a young age to help their mother make ends meet.

Grandpa Glen soon returned, and Grandma Mamie took him back. Nothing had changed, and the fighting continued. When the fights were really bad, Mom and her sister, Gerry, would bury the butcher knives in the backyard, in fear their parents might kill each other. When the fight subsided, the girls hurried to wash them and return them to the kitchen drawer.

While Grandma Mamie was at work one day, Mom and Aunt Gerry found a suicide note left in a kitchen cupboard…just in case.

In fear Grandma had taken her life, they ran to the bus stop and waited eagerly for her to return from work. Their hearts grew heavy as each streetcar came and went, but she was not on it. Finally, she arrived. The girls never let her know they had found the note.

Dad wanted desperately to rescue her out of there, and she wanted desperately to be rescued. He saw in her a young woman who wanted stability, to be loved and cared for. He worried about the added heartache if he were caught and had to return to the chain gang, but determined to keep his life moving forward, he confessed that he was crazy about her.

"I'll buy you a fur coat! Just say you'll marry me, sweetheart."

It had only been a few months when they eloped. On the third day of July, 1941, she told her mother she was going to stay at a friend's for a few days. Instead, they met at the train station and made the hour-and-a-half ride to Baltimore to take their vows before a justice of the peace.

She was 16. He was 26. She lied about her age…he lied about his past. What they didn't lie about was how they felt.

Unsure how to tell her parents, Mom took off her wedding ring and went home like nothing had happened. At work he'd watch her flutter up and down the aisles until their eyes met. Both hearts would skip a beat. He'd wink. She'd blush.

After a few days, she went home once again to her parents arguing. Her dad threw a catsup bottle across the room and walked out mumbling, "Let Dee clean it up."

She went upstairs, put on her wedding rings, and called her newlywed husband to come get her. She packed everything she owned in one small suitcase…two blouses and a skirt her mother had made.

She came back down with confidence that her future was more promising than her past.

"Mother, I hope you'll be happy for us. We got married in Baltimore last week."

Poor Grandma probably wished she had a way out herself. "Well, I just wish I could've been there. You know I want the best for you."

Grandpa Glen was relieved to have one less mouth to feed. "Why didn't ya tell us? We would've given ya a party!" he mocked in his usual smart aleck tone, slurring each word.

They walked out of that basement apartment and shut the door on her father's drunken sarcasm and into their new life as husband and wife.

Mrs. Simms was out of town when Mom moved in, so Dad was unable to inform her he had taken a bride and moved her into his room at the boarding house.

"Mr. Wadsworth!" she bellowed. "You don't have a woman in there, do you?"

He hurried down the hall to head her off. "She's not just any woman. That's my wife!"

"My, things happen quickly around here! Well, I guess you have a marriage license to prove it then, don't you?" she suspiciously queried.

"Mrs. Simms, you look disappointed," he teased. "You're not jealous, are you?"

"Why, Mr. Wadsworth! I'm old enough to be your Graaaaa... your mother!"

She scuttled back down the stairs. "You'll have to find another place to live," she bellowed one last time. "I don't allow married couples. You know that's against my rules!"

They moved again. . . and again.

In childlike wonderment, Mom later told me, "Whenever your Dad left the room, I loved to look in his closet. I was so impressed that he had a hat to match every suit!"

By 1941, many men sported a broad-brimmed hat—a status symbol of the recovering economy and for my Dad, of his promising circumstances. From leaving home with only the clothes on his back, life was taking a turn in the right direction . . .except for the lingering shadowy figure that hovered — someone with authority to take him back to finish his time on the chain gang.

## SUSAN TAYLOR & TERRY HICKS

*"Neither a wise nor a brave man lies down on the tracks of history to wait for the train of the future to run over him."*
-Dwight D. Eisenhower-

By the end of the decade the economy was turning around, but sadly, at the expense of human lives. A new dictator was rising to power in Germany, and war with Europe was looming overhead.

As time flew by for the two young lovers, Japanese war planes flew towards an unsuspecting America, and as he fell deeper in love with her, thousands of miles away on the other side of the country bombs fell on the unprotected rows of battleships that lay in Pearl Harbor. They felt as if life had just begun, but soon learned that life had mercilessly ended for thousands of others.

The whole nation stood at attention as a solemn President Roosevelt spoke. "Today, December 7, 1941, a day which will live in infamy, the United States of America, without any warning, was deliberately attacked by naval and air forces of the Empire of Japan. As Commander-in-Chief of the Army and Navy, I have directed that all measures be taken for our defense. With confidence in our armed forces—with the unbounded determination of our people, we will gain the inevitable triumph—so help us God."

The streets were filled with fearful chatter as people rushed home to be with their loved ones and wait for news. All the restless energy of the 1940s had suddenly found an outlet. America was at war!

Unlike most conflicts in our history, this one was brought on by a direct attack on the United States. Americans were the good guys, and that gave them the courage and determination to risk their lives in the armed forces, to make sacrifices on the home front, and to press on to victory despite the heavy and heartbreaking cost.

As time marched on for thousands of soldiers marching across Europe to invade Poland, back in Gastonia time stood still. Bessie worked her ten-hour shift. When the dope wagon came through the mill at lunchtime, she often bought a packet of Goody's headache powder, opened the little cellophane packet, tapped the powder onto her tongue, then washed it down with a six-ounce bottle of Coke. Her head, like her heart, began to ache the night her son first left home and it never stopped. She went home every day and checked the mailbox hoping for a card or letter—news that her son was okay. For six years, she watched the newspaper for his name to appear that he had been captured and brought back. As they say, *no news is good news;* she scrolled each page, skimmed the obituaries and dropped the newspaper.

### February 24, 1942
### Final Rites for J.C. Wadsworth, Jr.
### Well-Known Young Businessman of Concord Died Tuesday Night After a Brief Illness

Funeral services were held for 47-year-old
John Cyrenius Wadsworth, Jr.
Serving as honorary escort were veterans
of the 113th Field Artillery with
which he served during the first World
War. Mr. Wadsworth, known to his
many friends as 'Jack,' is survived
by his wife, and a stepson.

That year and for several years after, Grandma listed herself in the Gastonia City Directory as "Bessie Kinley-widow of John." In her heart she must have believed that. They say *you never forget your first love*. Bessie and John shared the birth of four children and laid three of them to rest together. That's a bond not easily broken. He had married the doctor's daughter, and raised her son from a previous marriage, but he never had any other children.

Grandma still lived with Evelyn who was married and had kids of her own. They wanted to move to a house with a yard, but Grandma wouldn't leave the house on North Rhyne Street— the house where her son could find her if he came home.

Mom and Dad moved to Baltimore, then back to D.C., then to

Buffalo, New York, for a short time. That's where he made good on his promise to buy Mom a fur coat. Mom's parents had moved back to St. Louis, so Mom and Dad hitched a ride with a stranger going that way. People did those kind of things back then. At least she didn't jump in the stranger's car with her fur coat on. Dad had to make payments, so the store shipped it to St. Louis when it was paid for.

People moved around a lot back then; always chasing opportunities. They traveled light. No moving trucks, just packed up the car and left. For Dad there was an ulterior motive—not staying in one place long enough to be tracked down.

Coming on the heels of the Depression when millions could find no work, the war shook things up especially economically. Factories were transformed by private companies from civilian to wartime production and operated on triple shifts to make airplane engines, tanks, bombers and guns. American industry shook itself from Depression-era slumber. Dad had a desire to see California, so he headed west to Fresno, secured a job, then sent for Mom. She said it rained every day they were there and she hated it, so when her family relocated to Las Vegas, and Grandpa Glen sent word that he could get Dad work there in an ammunition plant, they crossed yet another state line to make their home in Nevada.

While they were busy establishing their home in Las Vegas, the Allies were establishing their headquarters in London, and while the newlyweds made plans for their future, the allies were making plans to invade Nazi-occupied Europe.

While every American citizen was expected to participate in Home Front efforts, a sense of patriotic duty called men and women to leave the comfort of home to fight for freedom. Still a fugitive of the law, Dad kept a low profile until the day he and Mom walked to the mailbox, excited to drop off the final payment on their trailer in Las Vegas, and pulled out his letter from Uncle Sam. He opened the letter slowly, as if by so doing, he could somehow delay the inevitable. Together they stared at the official document while each read silently:

*April 21, 1943*
*Royal Scott Wadsworth,*
*You are to report to active duty in the United States of America's Armed Forces, and to serve for the duration of the war.*

> *"In the final choice a soldier's pack is not so heavy a burden as a prisoner's chains."*
> -Dwight D. Eisenhower

Staring at the crumpled draft notice, he breathed in a deep breath, then let out a sigh of relief. The notice that brought panic for what the future might hold is the same notice that brought peace for what the past had let go of. He had been successful in changing his identity. At least the United States Army believed he was Royal Scott Wadsworth.

Working in the ammunition plant provided a 2-A military deferment, but when he gave up that job for one in construction, he gave up any excuse for not being in uniform. Within six months of the bombings at Pearl Harbor, every able-bodied young man not wearing the military colors was ostracized from society. He had evaded his duty long enough and was more than willing to serve his country in war time, however, he faced a unique dilemma. Everyone who enlisted knew they would be marching forward to the horrors of war. What frightened him was the added risk of marching backward to the chain gang.

He and Cousin Rube had battled with swords hand carved from sticks, dueling to the bitter end to see who would be king of the mountain. Something deep inside told him what he was about to encounter in the months to come would be far from make-believe.

The bus pulled in to the reception center in Utah, and lines formed for registration. Heads were shaved and arms inoculated. They were officially sworn in, issued the basic GI articles of clothing, and read the "Articles of War." He was now a soldier in the United States Army.

They were tested to see if they possessed any special skills, then assigned to their units by lining them up and dividing them into two groups. 'A' through 'R' was assigned to an infantry unit, and 'S' through 'Z' to the medical corp. It was the first time dad pondered if it would be better to be a Kinley or a Wadsworth, but that decision had been made. Before the dust settled on his boots, he was rounded up and on his way to Fort Benning, Georgia, for twelve weeks of basic training.

The new recruits swapped horror stories about basic training, comparing it to hell on earth. Those who didn't believe it coming in were believers on their way out. They clumsily marched around camp as a platoon of seasoned soldiers paraded by in perfect formation. The drill sergeant yelled an order, and the men dropped to the ground simultaneously for 50 push-ups.

They were serenaded by the cheerful epithets of a unit on their way out.

The wooden huts built by the first recruits to arrive looked as if they had been patterned after a hotdog stand from the county fair. Living in close quarters was reminiscent of the prison camp, although the character of most of these fellows seemed a much higher caliber.

The platoon sergeant was committed to teaching the new soldiers military discipline and accomplished his task by getting in their faces and screaming profanities at even the slightest of infractions…similar to the guard back in the chain gang, but this sergeant trained them to defend their freedom. The prison guard took pleasure in reminding the men daily that they had lost theirs.

They received classes in poison gas and practiced with bayonets. They marched around with wooden guns sawed out of 2x4s and were taught to shoot at a rifle range. They went through rigorous physical training, and the only thing that got him through were his thoughts of coming home to Mom.

One of the required induction classes was on sex education. This seemed to disturb a good many of the guys in the unit. A doctor displayed a collection of 35mm slides of some of his patients who had contracted syphilis and gonorrhea. He used a naked patient vividly exposing his body parts for all to see.

The unit was rousted early one morning before reveille sounded. Without time to wipe the sleep from their eyes, they were ordered to get ready for a "short arm inspection." Their eyes darted back and forth at each other, hoping someone could clue them in on what they were being ordered to do. Even more puzzling, they were told to line up wearing nothing but a raincoat and a pair of shoes. The Army doctor went up and down the line checking for venereal disease. The experience was humiliating. They felt pushed to the limit of what a man should endure physically, mentally, and emotionally, but with war raging in Europe and Japan terrorizing the South Pacific, they understood its purpose.

As the training heated up, so did the weather, and as basic training came to an end, so did the summer of 1943. It was now their turn to serenade the new recruits on their way in, as they were on their way out to Fort Sam Houston in San Antonio, Texas, for advanced medic training.

> *February 25, 1944*
> *My Darling Wife,*
> *I am so lonesome. I thought it would help some by writing you. Hope you are getting plenty of sleep and your work isn't too tiresome. Oh sweetheart, I will be so glad when the war is over, and you can quit work for good. I will be very happy when I can come home from work and you will have me a nice meal cooked. Darling I really like your cooking a lot.*
> *Darling I certainly feel sorry for a good many fellows here. Most all of the boys seem to talk a lot about what they are going to do after the war is over. It sure is a pity that so many lives are torn up over the war. However considering that so many have been killed, I suppose most of us are lucky. Anyway I feel so sure that it is about over until I hardly can think different. Dolores I have been talking to quite a few of the fellows here and some of them have been married 4 and 5 years and don't have any children so I suppose you and I are just about average. I was just thinking last night. If we should have a baby boy, you want to name him Rodney? That name starts with the first letter of my name. Wouldn't it be nice if we would have his*

*middle name start with a 'D' after you? What do you think about it? There are quite a few nice names that start with 'D'. There is Daniel, David, Donald.*

*Oh Sweetheart, it would be so wonderful if we would have a sweet little baby. I would really be happy.*

*Dolores darling, I think about you most all the time. The Lord must have seen that we were meant for each other. It seems funny at times at the way we got married. I am really glad it happened that way. We have been through some very rough spots together and I feel that we are closer than ever before. Darling, I have always loved you. After I came home on leave, I believe my love for you hit an all time high. I would travel around the world for you, and that's putting it mild.*

*Darling, I still have you pictured in my mind of how you looked that night we went to the Roosevelt Hotel. Darling you were really beautiful and I knew beyond any doubt that I was madly in love with you. Sweetheart if you only knew how you make me feel when you kiss me with those sweet tender lips.*

*Darling, I really feel so happy when we are alone. I can sleep so good when I am near you. So Sweetheart tell the family hello and I sure miss them a lot. Be sure and write me lots of nice letters. Remember I love you very, very much, so pleasant dreams to my sweet little baby.*

*Love and Kisses, Roy*

A Western Union delivery man rode his bicycle through Gastonia to inform families whose loved ones were wounded overseas. While Bessie worried, watched the news, and waited for mail wondering if her son was okay, Mom continued to receive letters.

*March 7, 1944*
*My Darling Wife,*

    Received two very sweet letters from you yesterday. Didn't have time to answer them last night, so will do so today. Darling your letters really make me so happy, and I enjoy them so much.

    I suppose you were glad to see your father home again. Am sorry to know he didn't land a good job. Perhaps things will pick up a little in St. Louis this spring. Sure hope so anyway.

    Darling I really think it is so sweet of you to kiss my picture every night. I am so very lucky to have a sweet girl like you for a wife. Darling it makes me so happy to know you love me that way. I sure love for you to write and tell me how happy you are. Darling I have always wanted you to be just like you are now. Darling I feel that you are the most perfect wife in all the world and sometime soon I am going to make you the happiest woman in all the world. Darling from now on I am really going to treat you like a baby. I am going to do everything possible to make you happy. Sweetheart I am so glad we both realized just how much our love meant to each other and how wonderful it is for two people to love one another. Really Dolores, I depend on you for so much. If I should ever lose you my life wouldn't mean much to me.

    Dolores when you wrote in your letter that you would always be happy with me whether we took a walk thru the park, spent the evening at home, or went to a movie, that was such a wonderful thought. Really darling, those kind of little things mean so much to me. Darling you know when I feel most content is when I am sleeping close to you with my arms around you. I sure think of those wonderful memories so often.

    The picture of the bridge where I first kissed you is a picture I prize very much. I remember so plain the afternoon I took those pictures. I was very lonely and decided to finish taking a roll of film that I had started. Little did I realize that 3 or 4 years later I would kiss the most beautiful little girl in all the world. Life does have a lot of strange things. You can bet your life that picture of the bridge means a lot to me, or should I say us. I can remember that day so plain. You pretended you didn't want me to kiss you, but I believed different. I also remember us going by The Toddle House on Ga. Avenue. I was so proud to have the boys see what a cute little trick I had. Remember the Sunday afternoon you met me at The Toddle House? I can still picture how beautiful you looked in that yellow dress. Really Dolores I have always liked the way you are built. I sure think your legs are really something to look at. I suppose you think it rather silly for a guy to talk about his wife this way. Darling I am really crazy about you and I don't care who knows it.

Dolores about us having some children, I don't care very much if we don't have any until I get out of the Army. I feel like you do. You can be sure we will have the sweetest little babies in the world when I come home. Darling I would give anything to see you holding one of our babies. I would be so happy. I don't know what I would do.

Darling I don't think it will be much longer before I come home. The war news looks better every day. I was reading in the papers where soon as Germany was knocked out they would start discharging quite a few married men from the Army. So that is some encouragement.

The pictures you have at home are not any of the boys in that truck accident. That sure was a terrible thing to happen. They are much more careful at driving now.

Well Dolores darling, I suppose you are tired of reading so much. I was lonesome for you and just kept sitting here writing away. Tell the family to be good and write when they can. You be a good little girl for me. I am glad the picture looks good now and about being scared in the house, you should have a lock on the door leading up to the apt. Ask the landlady to get you one. There is a *house full of people there and of course you are safe, however I know how you feel being by yourself.*

*Well Sweetheart when you kiss my picture, please think of me. Thanks for the kisses. Write real soon, and a lot of pleasant dreams to my sweet little wife.*

*XXOOOOOOOXX Worlds of Love and Kisses Roy*

By June, Dad had earned enough points for a furlough and was on his way home. Mom and her sister had remained in Utah waitressing for a while, but when their parents relocated back to St. Louis, the girls soon followed. Grandpa Glen left for Egypt to work for two years, so like many homes in America at that time, the women were holding down the fort. It was a full day of travel, only one day at home, then back to the train station saying their goodbyes once again.

The primary question on every soldier's mind was not only when he would be sent out, but where would he be sent—Europe or the Pacific? It wasn't that they were in a hurry to get there. They were just in a hurry to get it over with.

October 12, 1944, the announcement came. Their unit had been called up, and they would be leaving the next day. Dad was assigned to the 459th Medical Corp. He walked up the gangplank and entered the overcrowded ship—destination, Europe. As they were shipping out, the men stood on the deck of the Queen Mary, realizing they were leaving everything they knew behind and wondering if their tickets were round trip or one way.

A parade of Coast Guard boats escorted them safely down the

Hudson River and out into the Atlantic before the Coast Guard circled back and the soldiers were on their own. The Queen Mary had once been considered the grandest passenger ship ever built, but with the outbreak of World War II, she was transformed into a troopship overnight. The luxurious furnishings were removed, the indoor pool was drained, and bunks for the soldiers were added everywhere possible. She was built to carry 3,000 passengers, but as a troopship, she had over 15,000 men aboard. The exterior was painted black and the windows were blacked out so the enemy couldn't detect lights. Even the ash from a lit cigarette was forbidden out on deck at night. Because she zigzagged through the water like a spirit in the dark, the soldiers referred to her as "The Gray Ghost." She carried them safely through the cold Atlantic waters to another continent a world away from what they knew. Upon landing in Southampton, England, many of the men were sicker than dogs and happy to be back on soil, even if it was foreign. They were physically prepared and mentally ready to do their part to fight the enemy…or so they thought.

The romance and urgency of men shipping off to war had couples rushing to wed and conceive children. While Dad was crossing the high seas, a letter from Mom waited on the other side. *They had a "furlough baby" on the way!*

*"Our pleasures were simple—they included survival."*
-Dwight D. Eisenhower

By the time they arrived in Europe, the writing was on the wall for the Axis powers. The economic strength of the Allies was growing day by day, and there was no doubt in anyone's mind, the Allies were winning. That is, if you can call death and destruction around every turn winning.

Dad's last eight years' survival depended on not being noticed. Now as a medic, or aid man, as they were called, he wore a red cross on his armband and one on his helmet calling attention and identifying himself to wounded men seeking treatment. According to the Geneva Convention, the cross was supposed to keep the enemy from firing at them. They were warned, however, the bright red cross actually acted as an enticing target for many enemy soldiers.

The beautiful green countryside now void of the once-vibrant colors of life became hues of black and gray. Cities were reduced to mere rubble and people's lives destroyed. The sights were more than any human eyes should ever see; things that haunted many men for the rest of their lives.

The medics' job was not to perform extensive treatment of the wounded, but to stabilize them. They were trained to stop bleeding, apply sulfa powder on wounds as an antiseptic, apply dressings, and administer morphine as a sedative. The medics often had to make the decision of which wounded soldiers were beyond help and when to move on to retrieve fallen soldiers who had been blown apart but had a chance and transport them in the ambulance to the nearest field hospital. Some lived. Countless others did not.

In Germany, our troops were fighting an enemy that was defending their homeland. Fields were planted with terrifying weapons designed to detonate at testicle height with a lethal shower of steel balls and steel fragments exploding in all directions. British soldiers called them Debollockers. Bollock is slang for testicles. The Allies adopted nicknames like *The Bouncing Bitch, The Castrator* or *Bouncing Bettys*. The psychological effect was great.

Amidst the bombs dropping, Dad waited anxiously for news from home. The baby was due in March. Being surrounded by so much death, he needed desperately to be reminded life still existed.

The Army had done a good job training the men physically to perform their job, but how do you prepare mentally to see the man who slept in the bunk next to you writhing in agony, his stomach opened up and his guts spilling out? Bombs exploded with loud claps of thunder as men fell like drops of rain. Motion was crippled by the thick smoke. The landscape, shades of black and gray splashed with red—bright, unmistakable crimson red—the spilled blood of men. The screams of the wounded and dying echoed through the haze from all directions. Confusion became chaos. The stench of death was everywhere.

Mom's due date was now past, yet still no word from her. The Germans were fighting until the bitter end as the troops continued on the move with the Allies closing in from every angle.

It had been four long years since the war began. Many of the soldiers were suffering battle fatigue. They evacuated and treated a good number of men who were exhibiting symptoms of severe psychological damage that affected them for years; in some cases, for the rest of their lives.

By April the letter finally arrived from Mom announcing that March 20th they became the proud parents of an 8 pounds, 2 ounce, 20" long baby girl. They had agreed on a 'D' name like hers, but Donna Lee had blue eyes like his.

The beginning of May brought the beginning of the end for Hitler and his Third Reich. On May 7, the German forces surrendered unconditionally to the Allies. The war was finally over in Europe. Now that the hostilities had stopped, they all took a deep breath and tried to relax.

*May 18, 1945 Peine, Germany*
*My Darling Wife,*
*Received several letters from you and enjoyed hearing from you very much. Am getting along fine, and hope all of you are the same. We sure are having exceptionally nice weather now. Everything is so nice and green. I would give anything to be home with you and the baby. However, I suppose that will be some time yet. I only have 48 points, so therefore will have to wait and hope*

for the better.

I had the baby's bracelet and locket finished. They sure look nice. Will send them home soon. The locket is made from a Russian coin and the bracelet from German and Polish coins. They will make nice keepsakes for her.

Well, we are allowed to tell our location here in Germany now. The town we are in is Peine. The town is one of the few in Germany that has not been blown to bits. The houses here are very modern. We live in a nice house with hot water, gas and lights. We have a nice place to do our laundry. Peine is about twenty miles from Hanover, on the the Auto Bown highway. It is also near Brunswick. The farm land here is very good. The people all have real nice gardens and take great pain in working them. We are not allowed to talk to any Germans. If a soldier is caught talking to a German, he is court-martialed and fined $65. There is quite a large German hospital here in town. It is full of wounded German soldiers. The town is also full of Russians, Polish, and Italians who were slave labor under the Germans. The people all over Europe are really starved. I think Germany is far better off in the food and clothing question than any other European country. The German people seem to be very hard-working people, and a lot of them are most likely glad the war here is finally over.

While in England, I was stationed in a school at Ulverston, England, the birthplace of Stan Laurel. The town was about 10,000 pop. and about 8 miles from Barrow. Barrow is an aircraft carrier and submarine repair base. Barrow was bombed quite a bit during Englands black moments. Ulverston was blacked out at night and it was quite difficult to find your way around at first. They had two nice movies there. I think you have the snapshots of England. I had the opportunity to visit Lanchester. It was quite interesting visiting there. Also went over to Malcolm Bay. That is a big summer resort. It was sure cold and windy that day, so I didn't stay long. We moved by motor from Ulverston to South Hampton England. So we had the opportunity to see a lot of the countryside of England. We spent the night in a British Army camp. I tried to get postcards along the way, however as we were in a convoy that was impossible.

The boat ride from the States was really tiresome. We spent about 12 days on the water. I only got sick one time. The water was very rough and choppy for about 3 days. The boat had plenty of books to read and a movie every night. We were not allowed out on decks at night and not allowed to smoke during the night. The boat ride across the English Channel wasn't so bad. It took us about 3 days. We layed over quite awhile a ways out from South Hampton. We landed in LaHavre, France. Boy that place has really been shelled. We went by motor from LaHavre to Camp Twenty Grand, near Rouen, France, and from there to a small French Village, Gespert, near the Belgium border.

The newspaper clipping I sent you is the pontoon bridge where I crossed the Rhine River. We're in Waldrich, near M. Gladback. M. Gladback was really knocked to pieces. We were only 7 miles from the Ruhr pocket when it fell. I was also in the castle at Rheda, Germany. You most likely read in the papers of the beautiful castle there. Our company is working with a field hospital handling shell shocked or battle exhausted cases whichever you prefer to call it. At times we had quite a few cases and I sure feel sorry for those boys. We got our E & O ribbon and the battle star for the Battle of Germany today.

I have a nice German sword and a lot of German Army badges. I am going to try and get sent home. Also, German, Polish, and Russian money. I have your father a very good German lugar. It is a 1917 model. It has a very long barrel which can be cut down if he prefers. It has an elevated sight. It is 8.82 and has firing power capable of killing anyone at 300 yards. It is one of the best guns made. We are not allowed to send pistols home. I packed the gun in *a lot of white Vaseline and wrapped it in wool cloth and paper. We have to turn guns in to our supply and they give us a record signed by our captain. The gun will be very nice to take on hunting trips.*

*Well Dolores, I sure hope everyone is getting along nicely. Give all my love to our darling baby. Be sure to send the snapshots soon as they get back. Give my regards to everyone. Remember darling, I am always thinking of you. I miss all of you very much. A world of love and kisses to a very darling wife and bundles of love to Donna Lee.*

*Lots of Love, Roy*

*PS Enclosed is some stamps for you, Mother, and Gerry.*

We lost over 400,000 American soldiers in the war. About 670,000 men were wounded in battle. Close to 140,000 servicemen were taken as prisoners of war, and countless others were scarred for life. Freedom had been secured. Some would argue the price was too high, but not Dad. He knew when he laid his head down at night he could sleep in peace knowing Donna Lee would continue to live in a world where she was free to let her dreams take her as far as she wanted to go.

# Chapter 18

*"The real and lasting victories are those of peace, and not of war."*
-Ralph Waldo Emerson

The end had arrived. The new beginning welcomed it. Hope reigned in the hearts of people that peace would rule the land. For four long years our soldiers fought bravely, our people endured hardship, and our nation prayed for victory. The world listened with joy on May 8, 1945, as British Prime Minister Winston Churchill confirmed that the German high command had met with Allied officials and signed surrender papers.

Churchill's familiar, grandfatherly voice crackled out across the airwaves, "The German war therefore is at an end."

On August 14, 1945 President Truman stepped before eager

reporters in his White House office and announced the surrender. In New York City's Times Square, half a million people who had gathered in eager anticipation of such an announcement went into a tizzy when the board on the New York Times Tower flashed the long-awaited news, "Official—Truman announces Japanese surrender." Within three hours, another one-and-a-half million frenzied New Yorkers joined their fellow citizens in Times Square. Clubs, bars, and restaurants filled to overflowing with excited patrons who drank, sang, and toasted the fall of Japan. Almost lost in the din were those reflecting somberly on lost brothers and sisters, fathers and mothers, husbands and wives, and sons and daughters.

In Washington, D.C., 10,000 delirious residents gathered across from the White House in Lafayette Park where they celebrated wildly. Music blared, people sang, and soldiers, sailors, and civilians danced happily across the park in a long conga line.

At eight p.m., the president answered as the people cried out, "We want Truman!"

Walking out onto the White House's north lawn, he took in the scene with a smile, then spoke: "Ladies and gentlemen, this is a great day. This is the day we have all been looking for since December 7, 1941. This is the day when fascism and police government ceases in the world. This is the day for democracies. This is the day when we can start on our real task of implementation of free government in a world where we are faced with the greatest task we've ever been faced with. The emergency is as great as it was on December 7, 1941. It is going to take the help of all of us to do it. I know we are going to do it."

Dancing and singing broke out from England and France to New Zealand and Australia. Parades rolled through the streets. The long horror was over. It was time to celebrate. American soldiers scattered across the globe let loose. Scores of GIs stationed in England went wild in London's West End, tramping gleefully through streets with the Stars and Stripes and bellowing at the top of their lungs, "Yankee Doodle Dandy."

In a solemn ceremony aboard the Battleship Missouri, General Douglas MacArthur spoke and called for a new era of peace in the Pacific. He saluted the millions of Americans who had fought to win the peace and praised American families that had persevered and worried for years while their loved ones fought overseas.

He voiced the words they longed to hear, "They are homeward bound—take care of them."

Word finally arrived at the beginning of September. They would be shipping out in a few days. They turned in their gear—rifles, gas masks, helmets, gun belts, and bayonets, which made the load they carried home much lighter than the load they carried over there; not just physically, but mentally, too.

General Patton reminded them, "It is foolish and wrong to mourn the men who died. Rather, we should thank God such men lived."

Dad sailed home on the Queen Elizabeth. The once-pristine luxury liner proudly bared her battle scars of a long and hard-fought war. The five days of travel gave time to ponder the past. Images of an early morning attack when a GI still in his teens stepped on a mine and had his limbs blown off, caution of avoiding them himself, laying in cold, damp trenches, crawling to the front lines to carry wounded soldiers out of enemy gunfire, the urgency driving the ambulance while a comrade's blood left a trail.

Heading across the Atlantic, the morale on the ship was extremely high, and there was a smile on every GI's face preparing for the unique challenges each would face as they reentered civilian life. The only complaint uttered was while they were on the fastest ship on the ocean at that time, it wasn't getting them home fast enough to see their loved ones. Everyone was ready to make the adjustments to peacetime.

Eventually the fog began to dissipate and the sun broke through. The ship's whistle blew, and the sound brought screaming soldiers pouring in from every direction. Hearts pounded with excitement.

They stood on deck and watched together as the breathtaking view of the New York skyline came back into sight.

A multitude of voices pointed out familiar landmarks, but it was the Statue of Liberty which stood tall and proud, holding her torch for all to see as she welcomed them home. A hush swept across the crowd and the men stood awestruck as the ship sailed by her preparing to dock. It seemed as if she were speaking to them.

They strained to hear her whisper, "Well done, boys. Well done."

When they arrived, there were no huge celebrations like the first soldiers returning home had received. The cheers had long since faded, but there were still plenty of family members anxiously waiting for their returning loved ones. Walking off that ship was a lot easier than it had been walking on. Many of the guys exited the ramps, knelt down on all fours, and kissed the ground. The troops poured into New York's Grand Central Station to board trains homeward bound.

Jefferson Barracks, affectionately referred to as the freedom center, was Dad's point of separation. He received his three hundred dollars in mustering pay and was honorably discharged from the Army. He had worn the uniform of the United States of America with great pride, and knowing this would be his last time to button up the jacket and slide the cap over his head evoked mixed feelings.

Families reunited. Returning soldiers reentered the workforce. Most women left wartime work to return home and concentrate on childbearing and child rearing, and a Baby Boom followed. They built homes, lovingly raised record numbers of children, and transformed America into an economic and military powerhouse with unparalleled global influence. People became more optimistic and looked forward to the future.

Dad could still smell the fumes from the ship that carried him home. He still heard the screams of dying men and felt the fear of those he served side by side, but like the rest of his past, he buried it and never spoke of it again.

## Chapter 19

> *"I don't measure a man's success by how high he climbs, but how high he bounces when he hits bottom."*
> -General George S. Patton

World War II blew away the Depression like an uninvited storm. Now that the war was over and the dark clouds cleared, the sun began to shine on the glory days. Technology expanded, the automobile industry was back in production, and single-family houses were mass produced in the suburbs.

Americans were anxious to purchase cars, homes, and other luxuries denied during the war, and Mom and Dad were no exception. He worked days landscaping and nights as a security guard at a chemical plant to give his new family every advantage he never had.

Making good on his second promise to Mom, they took advantage of his G.I. bill and bought a little home with a white picket fence in Carsonville, a suburb of St. Louis. Living the American dream was becoming reality, until living a lie interfered.

Fugitive officer J.S. Braswell came all the way from North Carolina prepared to take him back to finish the two years in the chain gang that he had escaped.

Does Roy Kinley live here?" Braswell asked Mom.

She assured him she knew no one by the name of Kinley. Dad arrived home and entered the house like the unsuspecting prey of a cat on the prowl.

"Roy Kinley?" Braswell questioned.

The name hit him like a punch he couldn't block—the name he abandoned over a decade ago.

The fingerprint system was fairly new and the FBI was now doing random fingerprint checks against the army's records. After eleven years of looking over his shoulder, Royal Wadsworth, husband, father, veteran, law-abiding citizen was exposed for the first time to our mother as Roy Kinley, fugitive from a chain gang. She had no clue about what was happening as St. Louis Chief of Police took Dad into custody.

Mom had no resources or connections, but sympathetic police officers convinced Morris Shenker to take Dad's case pro bono. Shenker was a young lawyer with a reputation as a mover and a shaker. He was a Jewish immigrant from Russia, a financial genius who knew people in high places.

Playing out each scenario like a hand of poker, Dad wasn't sure if it was time to up his ante or to fold. His world had come to a screeching halt, but as the morning light crept in, he was reminded the earth was still turning on its' axis, and outside those walls the policeman was still walking his beat, the doctor was treating his patients, the postman was delivering the mail, and eight hundred miles away, a taxicab driven by Dad's cousin Ruben sped down a country road with great urgency. His tires squealed as he made the last curve around the bend which led to North Rhyne Street.

"Aunt Bessie! Aunt Bessie! Have you seen the paper?" Cousin Ruben yelled, as he skipped every other step, bounced across the porch, and rushed through the front door out of breath.

His entrance brought the whole family running. "What's wrong, Rube? Is someone dead?"

"No," he said shaking open the paper. "Someone's alive!"

They all read the headlines,

## CAROLINA CHAIN GANG FUGITIVE CAPTURED IN ST. LOUIS AFTER 11 YEARS.

Morris Shenker came bright and early the next morning to meet with my dad and discuss his past, present, and future. Letters poured in to Governor Donnelly's office from family, friends, employers, and commanding officers in the medical corp attesting to Dad's character and begging for clemency.

The extradition hearing was set for April 10th at Missouri's State Capital. Officer Braswell attended, prepared to escort Dad back to North Carolina to finish his sentence. Braswell made his case before the Honorable Judge Thatcher. When he finished, he took his seat, confident that he had done everything needed to win his case, but he had underestimated his opponent.

Mr. Shenker boldly delivered a sincere and heartfelt message in his thick Russian accent, "Your Honor, I have reviewed this case fully and thoroughly. Let it show that the defendant Mr.

Kinley is now Mr. Wadsworth. I beg the court to look at this man who sits before us and see what I have come to know. This is a man, who along with a name change has changed his ways. In his youth, he chose the wrong path, but he was misguided by his environment. I make no excuse for the wrong actions of my client in the past, but I feel strongly that any criminal behavior is just that—in his past."

"Counselor, we are not here today to retry the original crime," Judge Thatcher cautioned. "We are here today to determine whether or not this man should be extradited back to North Carolina to finish out a sentence in which he has not completed."

"Yes, Your Honor, but it is my belief that when people feel that they have no choices, often they make wrong choices, and Mr. Wadsworth is no exception. His actions as a young man were wrong. There is proof that the conditions he was sentenced to in that chain gang were extremely harsh for his crime. So harsh that he risked his life and lost his family. Since then, he has led an honest life, with not so much as a traffic ticket. He served his country honorably as a medic in the United States Army in Germany, France, and Belgium. He distinguished himself receiving several medals for meritorious service. He now has a wife and a child depending on him for support." He pointed to Mom and two-year-old Donna on the front row. "Your Honor, I believe that often what prisons do is make criminals better criminals! Mr. Wadsworth has proven over the past eleven years that he knows how to live as a law-abiding citizen. I beg the court to answer this question: Would sending him back now serve any purpose?"

Judge Thatcher called for a short recess and retreated to his chambers.

Dad and Mr. Shenker rose as Judge Thatcher returned to announce his decision. "Having thoroughly reviewed your case, it is the opinion of this court," he paused momentarily and then continued, "to grant you clemency. The court has determined that you have rehabilitated yourself. You served your country in combat, and you are a self-supporting citizen. Clemency is only good in the state of Missouri. Should you travel outside the state, you could be returned to North Carolina."

The gavel pounded one final time and it was over. Not just the trial, but all the lies, all the years of looking over his shoulder, all his fears of getting caught. The dark cloud that hovered for over a decade faded away like a bad dream when morning comes. He was free. Free to resume life…as a husband, as a father, and soon…as a son.

## Durham Sun
## Durham, North Carolina
## April 14, 1947

**Congratulations**

Our congratulations to the Governor of Missouri and to Royal S. Wadsworth who owes to the Governor escape from a return to the North Carolina penitentiary.

Wadsworth is an escaper from a North Carolina prison camp. He got away in 1936. He had two more years to serve of a sentence for housebreaking. North Carolina located him and filed extradition proceedings to put him back behind bars. Governor Phil M. Donnelly has told North Carolina it cannot have the man.

Ordinarily, we would support the position that a robber should be returned to serve his time; but Royal Wadsworth's case is not an ordinary one. He has, Governor Donnelly finds, rehabilitated himself in the last 11 years. *That was the purpose of his punishment and the utmost that his prison sentence could do for him.* It would be stupid, now, to undue the making of the man. To demand his return now would be to take the position that *North Carolina justice is bent on vengeance not rehabilitation.*

Missouri finds that Wadsworth served in the Army with a good record, that he has established a family, a wife and a child, and that he has become a self-supporting citizen of St. Louis. Those things being true, without the least disloyalty to North Carolina, we are glad Missouri will not deliver him unto our prison authorities. We don't believe North Carolina knew the facts when it asked for Wadsworth unless some one-track, narrow mind got all tangled up in the idea that he had to do his duty under the cold, insensate law.

We only regret that Royal Wadsworth's name had to be emblazoned publicly, making it more difficult for him to live down a mistake and forget an unpleasant past.

A letter arrived with a North Carolina postmark. His past was about to meet his present.

# Chapter 20

> *"His heritage to his children wasn't words or possessions, but an unspoken treasure, the treasure of his example as a man and a father."*
> -Will Rogers Jr.

The return address on the envelope read *Evelyn Mills, Gastonia, North Carolina*. The sweet news that her brother was alive and well turned sour when he didn't immediately reach out to their mother. Nine long years passed since he last snuck home. Evelyn witnessed firsthand their mother's pain as she checked the newspaper and mailbox each day hoping for word that her son was safe.

Evelyn took it upon herself to write to the Governor of Missouri to ask for her brother's address and Governor Donnelly responded.

She wrote to her brother, *Mama needs to see you! We're bringing her now!*

Mixed emotions flooded like a faucet that wouldn't shut off, and they ran both hot and cold. The feelings were quickly drowned by the reality that he had abandoned them for so long.

Mom often used the saying, *if looks could kill* . . . That describes Aunt Evelyn's face in the photos taken at that bittersweet reunion. There's a feeling when your loved one caused you to worry. When you find they're okay you're not sure whether to strangle them or hug them and not let go. Grandma Bessie probably felt both.

*Dad & Aunt Evelyn*

Leaves fell, snow blew, flowers bloomed, mosquitoes swarmed, and Grandma Bessie came to visit every summer. There's a photograph taken of her back at her home on the sofa where she waited all those years for word that her son was alive. On the table, a photo of her granddaughter and the son she lost for eleven years. On her finger she wore the ring John gave her when he left for war. On her face she wore the signs of hard-fought battles of her own.

*Bessie*

The 1950s were happy days! Our family doubled with three more daughters. Industry was flourishing and the economy was booming. Jobs were plentiful. America was a land of opportunity. Americans who had just survived two decades of economic depression and war left the cities for greener open spaces of the suburbs where builders mass-produced affordable "cookie cutter" houses on the outskirts of cities. Suburban towns sprang up like crab grass across the country. People felt the need for security and family, so a baby boom and the suburban boom went hand-in-hand—the perfect family, a secure job, and a house in the suburbs. Fast food restaurants, drive-in movies, a television set in the living room, and an oversized car in every garage. Dad worked two jobs to make sure we had it all, and instilled in us *where there's a will, there's a way*.

Our home displayed a mongram 'W' on the awnings in front. By the driveway stood a black iron post with the name 'Wadsworth.' It was more than a name. It was a reminder of the father he never really knew and the man he chose to become.

In the 50s and 60s, before Civil Rights, our community was segregated. People of color were not even allowed to walk through our neighborhood, shop at our stores, or attend our schools or churches. Neighbors used derogatory names to speak about people of color, but our parents never did. When Dad served his time on the chain gang, 80% of the men he worked side by side and lived in close quarters with were black men. He never forgot that it was a black man who helped him escape. Like Dad, many of them were serving hard time for petty crimes. Dad didn't see skin color. He saw a brotherhood. Racial prejudice often seems to be inherited from one generation to the next. We saw that cycle broken in our home.

By the 1960s, Morris Shenker, the young attorney who represented Dad, became the most influential criminal lawyer in St. Louis history. He had a heart for helping wayward boys and partnered with Father Charles Dismas, a Jesuit Priest, to open The Dismas House, a shelter in St. Louis for ex-convicts re-adjusting to civilian life. *Hoodlum Priest*, a film released in 1961, was based on their story. Shenker co-owned the Dunes Hotel in Las Vegas and was fictionalized in the movie *Casino*. He became infamous for representing Teamster Boss Jimmy Hoffa and his association with the St. Louis Mafia. Good or bad, Mr. Shenker had what it took to secure Dad's clemency which gave him freedom as long as he never left the state of Missouri. We now understood why our family vacations took us to every corner of Missouri, but never crossed the state line.

North Carolina continued to punish prisoners, even ones who commited only petty crimes to serve their time in chain gangs into the 1970s.

Two of my sisters and I gave our sons and grandsons the middle name Scott in honor of our dad before we learned this was not his given name. It became even more special knowing it's a name that he chose himself when he turned his back on his past and became Royal.

Sitting around the dinner table in our middle-class home with a wife and four daughters, Dad's time on the chain gang never came up in our conversations. He never shared what it was like looking over his shoulder as a fugitive for eleven years. It would have been much easier if he had. He took the secret of his past to the grave, or so he thought.

*Susan, Royal, Donna, Dolores, Jenny, Terry*

> *"People will not look forward to their posterity,  
> who never look back to their ancestors."*  
> -Edmund Burke

## 2006

We turned left onto North Union Street in Concord where time seems to have stood still. The large, stately antebellum homes continue to create an impression of grandeur. A few dilapidated millhouses still standing, are now even worse for wear. This was where our journey began. Businesses have come and gone on South Union Street. The awnings have weathered and faded, but the old brick-front building that once housed Gibson's Drug Store still stands. I stepped inside, and our father's memory took a firmer hold on my heart. This yearning to know him better has been a journey filled with sentiment—a very rewarding sentimental journey.

On the back of one of Dad's photos is a handwritten poem by an unknown author.

*Have you ever seen a pathway stretching far ahead of you*
*That suddenly climbed a little hill*
*Then dropped away from view?*
*Then think of a path that's endless*
*Where your dear one is living still,*
*It's only we who cannot see*
*The path beyond the hill.*

*As little girls this picture of our dad intrigued us.*
*We always knew his strength*
*Now we knew the struggles he endured on his way to becoming Royal.*

# Author's Page

Susan Taylor and Terry Hicks, the co-authors of this memoir, are sisters. Susan lives on the West Coast and Terry is from the Midwest. They lost their father when they were in their teens and later discovered a secret about him that led to extensive research of the family's history and piecing together his incredible story through newspaper articles, official records, oral interviews, and travel to his hometown in North Carolina. Their vivid storytelling preserves the rich history and takes every reader back in time.